T5-ADM-627

TIME OUT!

Time Management Strategies for the Real Estate Professional

John M. Ravage

Real Estate Education Company
a division of Dearborn Financial Publishing, Inc.

While a great deal of care has been taken to provide accurate and current information, the ideas, suggestions, general principles and conclusions presented in this book are subject to local, state and federal laws and regulations, court cases and any revisions of same. The reader is thus urged to consult legal counsel regarding any points of law—this publication should not be used as a substitute for competent legal advice.

Publisher: Kathleen A. Welton
Acquisitions Editor: Patrick Hogan
Associate Editor: Karen A. Christensen
Senior Project Editor: Jack L. Kiburz
Cover Design: Sam Concialdi

©1991 by John M. Ravage

Published by Real Estate Education Company,
a division of Dearborn Financial Publishing, Inc.

All rights reserved. The text of this publication, or any part thereof, may not be reproduced in any manner whatsoever without written permission from the publisher.

Printed in the United States of America

91 92 93 10 9 8 7 6 5 4 3 2 1

Library of Congress Cataloging-in-Publication Data

Ravage, John M.
   Time out: time management for the real estate professional / by John M. Ravage.
   p.   cm.
   Includes index.
   ISBN 0-7931-0210-3
   1. Real estate agents—Time management. I. Title.
HD1382.R38 1991
333.33′068′8—dc20   90-23103
                                                                         CIP

Contents

Foreword   vii

Preface   xi

Acknowledgments   xv

Chapter 1. You *Can* Control How You Spend Your Time   1
Can You Really Manage Time? • Real Estate Agents Need To Manage Themselves • What Is Time Management and How Can It Pay Off? • The A, B, C... and D of Time Management • Controlling Events Means Creating Opportunities • The Life Cycle of a Real Estate Agent

Chapter 2. Decide What You Want—Today, Next Year, for Life   13
We Need To Control Our Power • The Power of Goals • Visualize What You Want Your Life To Be One Year from Now • Now Imagine Your Life in Five Years

Chapter 3. From Dreams to Goals to Action   29
Are They Your Own Goals? • Goals Change with Time • Translate Your Goals into Action

Chapter 4. Define Your Responsibilities   **41**
The Workplace • Family • Community • Allocate Time to Each Area of Responsibility • What Do You Have To Do?

Chapter 5. Create a System   **55**
Everything in One Place • Putting It To Work

Chapter 6. Plan Each Day's Activities, But Expect the Unexpected   **65**
Start with Your Goals • Meshing with Your Office's Systems • Make an Appointment with Yourself • When the World Won't Run According to Your Timetable • The Gentle Art of Saying No

Chapter 7. Match Your Performance to Your Goals   **81**
The 80–20 Trap • Start with a Time Log • Small Adjustment, Big Results • Analyzing and Adjusting Your Time-Use Performance • Conform the Real World to Your Ideal • You Are Now in Control

Chapter 8. The Urge To Procrastinate: How To Curb It; How To Use It   **97**
Why Do We Procrastinate? • What Does the Task Consist of? • Become an Expert Time Estimator • Procrastination Is Not Always a Dirty Word • Avoid Telephonitis and Other Interruptions

Chapter 9. What Is Your Time Worth?   **109**
Evaluate the Time Invested in Moving Up

Chapter 10. The Time-Managed Office   **113**
The Manager's Role • Turning Individual Goals into Collective Goals • Who's In, Who's Out? • Am I My File's Keeper? • Share the Nitty-Gritty or Assign It? • Tools of the Trade

Chapter 11. The Life Cycle of a Real Estate Agent   127
Primary Needs and Tasks Change with Experience • Not All Prospects Are Created Equal • Make a Commitment To Selling It Fast • Starting Out

Appendix   137

Bibliography   139

Index   141

Foreword

I first met John Ravage when he was writing an article about Weichert, REALTORS® for *Real Estate Business*. I am happy to see that he has now expanded the article into a book. No real estate professional can succeed without effective time management. And although we may disagree on some minor details, it is a pleasure to provide a foreword.

What Will Rogers very appropriately said about the significance of land can also be said of time—"They just ain't making any more." But on the bright side, we all have the same advantage. No one has cleverly created a way to add hours to the day. Success, like the value of land, appreciates profusely for real estate professionals who maximize each day's 24 hours—seven days a week.

I recognized early in my real estate career that whether you work alone, or run a 5,000-associate organization such as Weichert, REALTORS®, without time management, you can't be successful. In 1969, when I founded what is now considered to be among the top independent companies in the country, I bought a professional planning calendar and began making appointments with myself.

I never let a 15-minute block of time in my calendar go unfilled, whether I was making cold calls, reviewing listings, or completing paperwork. Today, as president of a 200-office company in five states and someone whose time is in demand, I still employ the same basic time-management technique.

I have long said that the real estate business is a simple one: not an easy one, but a simple one. The job is to bring buyers and sellers together, get them talking and close the transaction. The principle of time management in real estate is equally simple, and it's based on a commitment made when we agree to list and sell homes. Real estate is not a nine-to-five job; it takes 24 hours a day, seven days a week. The more networking, contacts and phone calls you make, the more business you do and the more money you make. Your level of professionalism is measured by the percentage of transactions you close and the amount of income you earn. You can make more contacts and increase marketing efforts by using your time wisely.

Here is my first rule of time management: Start your day earlier. Work from 7 A.M. to 9 P.M. Remember, I didn't say it was easy, I said the concept was a simple one—work longer hours.

By extending your hours, you increase the number of people you can contact. Real estate professionals have to be open for business when buyers and customers are not in business, and that means before busy people begin their jobs at 9 A.M., and after they quit for the day at 5 P.M.

Many frustrations and time-consuming games of telephone tag are eliminated by beginning work at 7 A.M. Phone builders before 7:30 A.M.; after that, they'll most probably be on-site and unreachable. If your buyer is a doctor or dentist, call before 8 A.M. when he or she is not with patients. Bankers' hours play a part in all of our lives—call them before 9 A.M. or after 3 P.M. Corporate clients are most reachable early in the day or late in the afternoon. This all adds up to getting up a bit earlier.

Here's strategy for the telephone-tag game, an unequivocal time-waster. We suggest that all our agents give more than just name and number when leaving a message. If you tell the receptionist or secretary what your call is about, you save time because the person can return your call with the answer you need.

My second rule is to make appointments with yourself. Avoid the common "to do" list, as it only takes up valuable time to compile. Instead, pencil in appointments and things to do right into your planning calendar. If you make a "to do" list, you have no way of knowing whether you've scheduled more tasks than you have time to do. Pencil is easily erasable in case the day's priorities and appointments change. When you break your day into 15-minute blocks and fill all the blocks, you know your day is complete. Anything left not done will have to be attended to tomorrow. You don't suffer guilt and frustration by not completing your "to do" list.

I plan my day in a fastidious fashion—setting appointments with myself for even personal details. If I want to schedule time to run, I block out an hour for myself. If I want to call an employee and congratulate him or her on a well-done project, I block out 15 minutes during the workday.

And no material on time management would be complete without addressing the omnipresent issue of paperwork. Paperwork is part of every business, and computer technology won't make it disappear. Real estate people must learn to make it as easy and convenient as possible. My rule is as easy as ABC:

A. Handle paper once and act on it. Either sign it, pass it along or discard it, but don't let it linger.
B. If the material is something you want to read but haven't the time now, file it and schedule time in your calendar for reading.
C. If it's junk, as much mail today is, scan it and relegate it to the trash.

Anyone who is serious about real estate should buy into the value of a time-management schedule. Those who are more committed may want to go a step further by analyzing the effectiveness of your system on a weekly or monthly basis. I recommend that all Weichert associates review appointment books and calendars. How much time was spent on prospecting? What marketing activities were more beneficial? What ideas did you institute to save time? Did you have a lot of unproductive time? Eliminating unproductive time is the single biggest improvement you can make in job performance. Never waste valuable time—your bottom line will feel it.

—James M. Weichert, President and
Founder, Weichert, REALTORS®,
Morris Plains, New Jersey

Preface

This book was written to help you sell more real estate. Yet it is not about selling real estate. It's about *time*.

More specifically, it is about time management—time management for the real estate professional.

As this is written, the prophets of doom are forecasting continued hard times in the real estate industry: declining housing starts; high interest rates; lower consumer spending. People are locked into their homes by economic conditions. It's the kind of market that puts an even higher premium on working smarter and devoting your time to the most rewarding activities.

Peter Drucker, the world-renowned management consultant, says that time is our most valuable resource. And he goes on to say that if time cannot be managed, then nothing else can be managed.

The Boston Consulting Group, in a series of monographs and in articles appearing in *The Harvard Business Review,* argues that time is "the next competitive resource." We'll look into that in some later chapters.

We often complain that there is never enough time. The Emperor Napoleon lamented, "Ask me for anything except time." We say, "If I only had the time," or "Time is running out." Or worst of all, "We ran out of time" when we have to explain why a certain task was not completed—or even begun.

The fact is that we all have exactly the same amount of time: 60 minutes in an hour, 24 hours in a day, 168 hours in a week. How we spend that time makes the difference between a good month and a so-so month. And the difference is cumulative. So-so months add up to so-so years; so-so years add up to a so-so career.

Few professionals work as many hours as real estate people. The median amount of time agents devote to their jobs each week is about 50 hours, according to the National Association of REALTORS®'s most recent survey. While many work fewer than 50 hours per week, an equal number works more than 50. And the median gross compensation among agents was $19,000 per year. Again that means that some earned less than the median, while an equal number earned more. Some earned *several times* the median. You probably know a few such stars. And it's a safe bet that those who earned the highest income weren't necessarily those who worked the longer hours.

You can be absolutely certain that those who earned three or four times the median income weren't working three or four times the median hours—150 to 200 hours per week. What made the difference? They weren't necessarily working harder; they were working smarter, focusing their time and their energy on the parts of their jobs that bring the greatest return. That's what time management is about.

If time is our greatest resource—and it's really the only resource a real estate agent has—then it pays to invest that resource as wisely as we can.

But, you ask, how can I control my time when I'm at the mercy of everybody else's schedule? I rise early and I run all day. I meet prospects after *their* workday, and that's often just the beginning of mine. I have 20 different things demanding my immediate attention. Before I can attend to the first one, the boss has a "little extra job" for me. And you tell me to take time to smell the roses.

Yes, it's demanding. But it can be a very rewarding life as well. You meet all kinds of people, and you have the opportunity to help them. You get the satisfaction of being a good matchmaker. Successful matchmaking brings the payoff—the financial and psychic rewards that justify the long hours of trudging, scrolling through the multilist computer, that make up for the disappointment of seeing the "perfect" house for your client sell before you even had a chance to show it.

As a real estate person, you have at least a dozen responsibilities—to your broker, your listings, your buyers, your family, yourself—and you have a dozen or more responsibilities under each of those headings.

The aim of this book is to help you evaluate your various responsibilities and organize them so that you devote an appropriate—and predetermined—amount of time to each of them, according to a thought-out plan that you have created to guide you through all the distractions that compete for your time. It is designed to help you concentrate on the activities that produce the greatest rewards, according to the values *you* have decided are most important to you. It will help you identify the time wasters that produce no rewards, and it suggests techniques to avoid them.

Time management can help you fulfill all your responsibilities and minimize the stress that comes from feeling you have lost control. It will help you develop an action plan that enables you to address your highest priorities, so that each day brings you closer to predetermined goals.

The real estate business is too varied and the people in it are too diverse to permit writing hard and fast rules for allocating your time to each of the many activities that make up your work week. No one can say, "You should spend 20 percent of your time working your farm, 20 percent telephoning prospects, another 20 percent showing houses, etc." Just as no budget can work for every household, no formula can tell you how much time to allocate to job, family, church and other responsibilities. Those are decisions you have to make for yourself.

Therefore this book offers no formulas, no rules that if followed will make you rich beyond your wildest dreams. It only offers guidelines that you can apply to your individual situation. It seeks to make you conscious of the value of time, to make you ask yourself, "Why am I doing this?" And to help you come up with a satisfactory answer.

The guidelines are extracted from proven methods to help you make the best possible use of your time—your most valuable resource—whatever your situation and wherever you are in your career. It can't cram any more minutes into each hour or more hours into your day. It can help you determine whether you are investing those minutes, hours and days to produce the greatest return. It will help establish an internal alarm that alerts you when you're wasting time so that you can take corrective action immediately and cut your losses.

Most chapters include an exercise designed to heighten your awareness of the value—and passage—of time and help you identify and organize your priorities. Do not feel you must complete each exercise before going on the next one, but do make a stab at it. Then go back and review your answers. Modify, add or delete as you gain insights into your needs.

Making the best use of your time does require effort and discipline. You will learn to deal with interruptions and reduce their number, frequency and duration. You will learn when to procrastinate, what to put off, and not feel guilty about it.

You will learn to reduce large tasks that seem unachievable into a series of smaller tasks that you can complete according to a schedule. Each successfully completed task will give you the energy to tackle the next task and the power to take on bigger challenges.

Probably the most important thing you will learn is that you can control how you spend your time. Once you have persuaded yourself that you are in charge of your time and your life, you will concentrate on the most rewarding tasks. You will concentrate on your goals and achieve them. And when you gain control of how you spend your time, you will find that there really is time enough for all the things you want to do—all the important things.

Good luck!

Acknowledgments

This book grew out of an article written for *Real Estate Business* based on the time management program of Weichert, REALTORS®, which is headquartered in Morris Plains, New Jersey.

Soon after the article appeared, I received a call from Wendy Lochner, then acquisitions editor of Longman Financial Services Publishing, to express interest in a book that would take real estate people through the entire process of setting, planning, and executing goals, and time analysis.

Without much hesitation I agreed, and then proceeded to miss my first deadline. Interviewing people and researching the practices of real estate agents across the country was a bigger undertaking than I had realized. An important rule of time management says, "Set ambitious goals that will stretch you." Another says, "If you're going to miss a target date, give advance warning." I stretched, gave advance warning and was kindly given a generous extension.

Therefore, my first thanks go to Wendy for seeing the possibilities and for extending the deadline. I also wish to thank Kathleen A. Welton, Publisher at the now renamed company, Dearborn Financial Publishing, Inc., who saw me through the process after Wendy returned to New York.

Another rule is, "Don't go it alone; get the help you need." This I also did and therefore wish to thank many people at Weichert who shared their valuable time and insights, in particular Sharon Sweeney, the "hero" of the *Real Estate Business* article; Philip Dezan, vice president; and James Weichert, founder of one of the most successful real estate businesses in the country and a self-acknowledged "nut on time."

My mentors in time management have been many, but two deserve special mention: Robert C. Dorney, cofounder and long-time president of Day-Timers, Inc. and Dr. Charles R. Hobbs, president of Time Power.

I especially wish to thank Bianca Franchi, a former Weichert trainer and manager, now of ReMax Executive Group in Morristown, New Jersey, whom I interviewed for the initial article. She encouraged me to undertake the book and suggested many investigative routes. She also agreed to read the entire manuscript, but only after returning from a long-planned, eight-week vacation with her son. Nothing could better illustrate the power of setting goals and priorities so there is time to enjoy the fruits of our labors.

I also thank my neighbors: Peter Paar for invaluable help in taming a frequently balky computer and Charles Hazzard, cobroker with Mopper—Stapen REALTORS®/Better Homes and Gardens, for reading selected sections of the manuscript.

If any errors, inaccuracies or confusions remain, they are my responsibility. In trying to write a book that recognizes the individuality of people, I may have drifted from some cherished precepts. Rather than prescribe hard-and-fast rules, I have described what works well in practice and attempted to show how readers can adapt these successful practices to their own needs.

I hope the result enables readers not only to increase their sales but also their enjoyment of life.

CHAPTER 1

You Can *Control How You* Spend *Your Time*

"Dost thou love life?" Benjamin Franklin asked. "Then do not squander time; for that's the stuff life is made of." And the wise Quaker went on to say, "Remember that time is money."

No one deliberately squanders time; yet we all do it. We start the day full of energy and good intentions, and at day's end we come to the sad, frustrating and stressful realization that we have accomplished none of the things we intended. We resolve to do better: "Come hell or high water, today I am going to call on that developer." Neither Satan's fire nor the flood occurs. Nor does the sales call.

Did we inherit a mischievous gene that leads us down the primrose path of procrastination? Have we no defense against interruptions? Are we so weak-willed that we cannot see every job through to completion?

If that were true, there would be little point in writing, much less reading, this book. The truth is that we all procrastinate occasionally. We sometimes welcome interruptions. We even interrupt ourselves. And we do drop tasks that grow tiresome or boring.

We should. There are times when procrastination is wisdom, and interruptions may turn out to be opportunities. When tasks prove unrewarding, we should cut our losses before squandering any more time.

Effective procrastination, keeping options open to seize opportunities and dropping unrewarding activities are all techniques to maximize your use of time. Collectively, these techniques are called time management, a somewhat misleading term as we shall see.

CAN YOU REALLY MANAGE TIME?

Can you change the length of the day? Can you make the clock tick more slowly? You can, but you would only be deluding yourself. You can even stop the clock, but that wouldn't change anything.

Time may seem to drag, or time may seem to gallop by. The fact is that time moves at its own pace. It slips quietly from the future to the present and becomes part of the past. "[N]or all your Piety nor Wit Shall lure it back to cancel half a Line...." Or a single second of time, the poet might have said as well.

You can't bottle time or freeze it and thaw it when you need a few extra hours. You can't put it in the bank, and you can't will it to your children. It is our most valuable resource, yet you have to spend it as fast you get it. The best you can hope for is to grab it as it comes and put it to the best possible use.

The important point to remember is that we all get exactly the same amount of time. Everyone's day is 24 hours long. Everyone's year is 365 days, with a little bonus thrown in every four years.

The answer to the question Can you really manage time? is that you can't—anymore than you can decide when the sun rises and sets. Or when the so-called selling season starts. But you can control the way you spend the time that's given you.

REAL ESTATE AGENTS NEED TO MANAGE THEMSELVES

Even though you probably work in a real estate office headed by a manager with years of experience in bringing buyers and sellers together, you still make the most important decisions about how you spend your time. You have to decide whether to meet Buyer A in Greenfield or try once again to get that listing in Northfield; to attend that meeting or make calls to your "listening posts" in various neighborhoods; or to work your farm or call on that developer.

Real estate agents are tied to other people's schedules. Buyers want to look at houses on weekends. Sellers are often out looking at their next house. People break appointments and leave a big hole in your day, which you may have trouble filling with the right kind of activities. And that can translate into a hole in your earnings. Still, you're the one who has to be flexible. You have to adjust to your buyers and sellers, regardless of what it does to your business or personal plans.

And that can lead to early burnout. A major cause of early burnout is the reward that doesn't measure up to the effort expended. For example, the average annual income of $19,000 for real estate agents working an average of 50 hours a week is hardly munificent. By learning to control how and where you spend your time, you can increase your return on time invested. You will learn to work smarter instead of harder. You'll be better able to roll with the punches. You'll learn to change directions smoothly and turn annoyances, like canceled appointments, into opportunities.

Who Is Wasting Your Time?

The first step is to be truthful with yourself. While it's true that some people waste our time—with or without our consent—we're pretty good at wasting it ourselves. We do crossword puzzles, leaf through the multilist book with no particular purpose or exchange war stories or rehash the weekend.

As a first exercise, write down the things you do of your own accord, without encouragement from anyone, that limit your productivity (List 1-1). On the opposite page, make a list of those time-wasting activities you engage in. There are suggestions in the above paragraphs; you can probably think of many more.

Don't be too hard on yourself. There's usually plenty of help available to help you waste time. So include time wasters that are urged on you, such as, "How about a cup of coffee?" Or the lunch that drags on when you had planned to work your farm or catch up on your telephone calls. Put them all down before going to the next page.

Isn't it amazing that we find so many ways to waste time? It's one of our most creative activities, and we invent new ones every day. We're going to do just the opposite; we're going to cut the list down to size.

Label the "wasters" you initiate. Go through your list and put your name or initials in front of the time wasters for which you are directly responsible. Nobody is asking you to do the crossword puzzle, so write your name opposite that entry if it's on your list. You are the perpetrator.

On the other hand, the office gossip can take a large bite out of your work time if he or she finds you particularly receptive. You're only an

List 1-1

Time-Wasting Activities Identified on _____(Date)_____
_____
_____
_____
_____
_____
_____
_____
_____
_____
_____

accomplice to that crime. So put down an "O," for "other," opposite this activity.

Now go back over your list and count the number of times your name appears and compare it with the number of Os. If your name appears frequently, you need to attack your work habits. That is your rogues' gallery.

If the Os outnumber your name by a significant margin, you have a slightly different problem. The goal still is to get control of your time. If people or events are imposing on your time, you have to take action. In a later chapter, we'll discuss some tactful ways to discourage people from wasting your time. And if tact doesn't work, we'll also explore some ways to deal with people who are a little short on sensitivity.

Redirecting your energies from self-initiated time wasters as well as those people bring to you requires a conscious effort. But it's important to realize that *you* can be in control. The temptation is to blame others or the manager or the system and ignore your own responsibility. That's the importance of this exercise: It reaffirms that you are in control—even for the negative consequences. In other words, you will convince yourself that no one really controls you or can make you do things you don't want to do.

Who Sets Your Working Hours?

Agents who work 60 to 70 hours a week are apt to say "I just can't get anything done in 40 or 50 hours." But who is forcing them to work those long hours? A professor of management at a large midwestern university suggests that "for the most part, a company isn't powerful enough to make a person work 60 hours a week if he doesn't want to." Many people do and enjoy it. Many others complain and promise their families that they will try to cut down. But they don't know how. They are not in control.

You should be able to decide how many hours you work. In real estate it isn't possible to say, "I work from nine to five, and come five o'clock, I'm outta here." You might be "outta there" for a long, long time. However, you can decide to work a specified number of hours each week. If an out-of-town client keeps you going until ten o'clock some evening, shorten the hours some other day. If you have set Wednesdays as midweek family dinner night, you can make that part of your regular weekly schedule: no Wednesday evening appointments. Or, if your family is flexible, you can change the night occasionally. What you are looking for is the maximum degree of control over how you spend your time at work and how you allocate your time between work and your personal life.

WHAT IS TIME MANAGEMENT AND HOW CAN IT PAY OFF?

One of the most widely respected time management consultants, Dr. Charles R. Hobbs, defines time management as the act of controlling events. Does that sound like a tall order? It is for many people. They perceive "events" to be things that happen to them, and they hope to react in time to at least escape serious harm. Notice the difference: acting or *re*acting. One is assertive and positive; the other is passive and negative.

Therefore, the first step in time management is to assert that you *are* capable of controlling the events that shape your life. Despite bosses, interruptions, emergencies and all the other distractions that nibble away at your life, you have to assert control over how you spend your time. You have the power to decide what you are going to do and you can develop the strength to do it.

Control comes with effort and determination. But it is also important to recognize those elements in our lives over which we have no control. Many of us could save ourselves a lot of grief and wasted time by heeding the words of the "Serenity Prayer": "God grant me the serenity to accept the things I cannot change, the courage to change the things I can, and the wisdom to know the difference."

We've already noted that the sun rises and sets according to an inexorable design, two events we cannot control. On the other hand, you can control the time you get up and the time you go to bed. You can control the number of hours you work each week, and you can control how you spend those hours.

But, you say, you just got through with the bad news that we, as real estate agents, have little control over our schedules. We have to fit our schedules to our clients and customers. We have to follow office routine, fulfill commitments, write all those dumb reports and spend all that time doing things that can't possibly produce a dime of income, much less pay for all the things we want for ourselves and those who depend on us. And now you say that we must control events.

Yes, you must control events or they will control you.

Want proof? Look around your office and ask yourself who the high-volume producers are. Some produce two, three or even ten times as much as the low-volume people. They control events. Ask them and they will probably tell you that they have developed a plan and a routine—a system—that helps them focus on activities that produce income. They organize their days and their weeks so that they accomplish their objectives.

The Search for Balance

Some do it almost instinctively. Somewhere in their lives, they set some goals and developed a plan to achieve them. For some, the plan was no more complicated than putting work ahead of everything else, and working as if the wolf was, if not at the door, coming around the corner. They work long hours and bring in many commissions. They live for their work.

Others decided that although work would be a major source of satisfaction—to say nothing of income—they would pursue other objectives simultaneously. They would seek balance in their lives. There would be children to enjoy, books to read, friends to cultivate, roses to smell. They recognized that although work would command a major portion of their time, it would not consume their lives.

So you will see high producers who start early and work late. Weekends are workdays. Vacations are unwelcome interruptions. Their spouses take responsibility for home and family. Some of these type-A personalities thrive on the pressure they generate and which drives them. Others wish they could get off the merry-go-round but don't know how. They've never learned to control their work. It controls them.

There are also big producers who move from appointment to appointment, bring in a fistful of listings each month and never seem to be out of breath. They have time to serve on committees and splash in the backyard pool. One such person aspires to be a scratch golfer, and she makes time each day to groove her swing.

Know What You Can and Can't Control

Real estate differs from most professions in that each person relies on his or her own efforts. What you do is what you get.

On the other hand, there are many things you *must* do, as we noted above. Meetings, open houses, caravans, desk time, waiting for late appointments to show up, all are part of every real estate agent's working life. And none relates directly to producing commissions. They just go with the territory. You have limited control over those events. But you can *plan* for them in most instances, so that they don't conflict with income-producing activities.

"Your" Time and "Their" Time

A certain amount of your time always will be claimed by activities over which you have little control. Let's call that *nondiscretionary* time—their time. It's time you can't control because someone is telling you, "You have to." What's left is *discretionary* time—your time, because it's time to use as you please, time to focus on your goals, time to work on the most rewarding activities.

We'll discuss discretionary time, its value, how to protect it and increase it in several subsequent chapters. What is important at this point is the difference between events you cannot control because they are scheduled for you and events you can control by scheduling them yourself; the time you spend because someone else controls that part of your schedule and the time you can devote to reach your goals.

Whether your discretionary hours are many or few, the important thing is to maximize their value by applying them to the most rewarding activities. You can squander them to nonproductive trivia, or you can devote them to working on tasks that have the highest potential for producing satisfaction.

THE A, B, C...AND D OF TIME MANAGEMENT

Most real estate agents agree that only activities that put you face-to-face with a prospective buyer or lister can generate income. We'll call time devoted to those activities "A" time. The more hours you spend face-to-face with prospects—buyers or listers—the more sales you will make and the more listings you will obtain.

But, for better or for worse, there's more to the real estate business than that. There are things you must do to position yourself to make a sale or secure a listing. You have to telephone for appointments, prepare presentations and generally serve your listings. Call that "B" time, because although these activities don't produce commissions directly, they are necessary preparations to or consequences of the face-to-face opportunities you seek.

Then there are all those other real estate-related activities—caravans, meetings, putting up signs, correspondence, updating records and so on—that cannot produce commissions. But they are necessary nonetheless. We'll call these "C" activities.

Professional development is an activity whose importance varies with individuals—their goals and where they are in their careers. Gordon Gundaker, a prominent midwestern real estate agent said, "Real estate is a profession that incorporates a great body of knowledge.... Constructing an attractive financing package, for instance, takes experience.... [T]he agent who understands the various alternatives and can present the advantages of each to the principals will attend more closings than the one who depends exclusively on the options offered by mortgage lenders" (as quoted in *Real Estate People,* Harper & Row). Find time for your professional development and assign to it a priority consistent with whatever stage in your career you happen to be.

Finally, there is "D" time for activities that do not relate directly to your real estate career. They, too, are important because first, they are part of the balance that time management seeks to achieve; and second, they frequently infiltrate your real estate work.

For instance, real estate agents can rise or fall on information. Who is moving? Who is building? Who is having a baby? Who got promoted? Who is bringing in executives? The more of that kind of information you acquire and apply to your work, the more listings and sales you will make. Activities that generate this kind of information depend to some extent on the individual, the territory and the broker. They also provide the opportunity to convert what appears to be low-reward "D" time to "B" or even "A" time if the casual contact turns out to be a prospect.

CONTROLLING EVENTS MEANS CREATING OPPORTUNITIES

For instance, a golfer may pick up a lot of leads around the club. If you do the family shopping, spend the time you stand in the checkout line to let people know you're in the real estate business.

As a real estate agent, you are almost totally dependent on your efforts. Although someone else may sell your listing, you got that listing largely by yourself. And if you make a sale, again it is by your own efforts.

Therefore, if your income goal for the coming year is, say, $50,000, only you can make it happen. You can't ask the boss for a raise or pray for a big Christmas bonus to offset the shortfall in commissions. You have to get out and secure the listings. You have to show houses to prospective buyers—after you have located the prospect and prepared a list of likely properties.

Ultimately, it comes down to doing what brings in the commissions —talking to prospective listers and showing properties to prospective buyers.

Let's look at that in terms of priorities, time and action. Everyone in real estate agrees that listings are the name of the game. If you get listings and serve them, you will prosper. Yet how many real estate agents have systematized their pursuit of listings? How many have calculated the value of each hour spent on the telephone talking to prospective listers?

The $15 Phone Call

Let's try to do that. If you're new in the business, you have to spend a lot of time on activities with relatively low and slow payouts, such as cold-calling. One successful manager figures it takes 100 cold calls to produce a listing. That's a lot of time and probably a lot of bruised ego.

Now translate those phone calls into time. If you set aside an hour each day for cold canvassing by phone, could you complete ten phone calls a day? That adds up to 50 phone calls a week—enough to secure that one listing in two weeks.

Going a step further, let's say that the average price for a home in your area is $100,000 and that the commission is 6 percent split evenly between listing and selling broker. If your broker splits the listing 50–50 with you and your listing was an average house, your share of the commission when it is sold will be $1,500, unless you have the good fortune to sell it as well, in which case your share would be $3,000.

But let's stick with just the listing commission. What did you do to earn that $1,500? You made 100 phone calls over a period of two weeks, devoting one hour a day to cold-canvassing by telephone. A total of ten hours for a $1,500 commission, which comes out to $150 per hour. At ten calls an hour, you come up with a value of $15 for each phone call.

We describe this example not to create visions of easy money. Cold-canvassing is hard work, and it takes skill as well as follow-up. But the numbers are valid, and they demonstrate the potential value of your time when you apply it to the right tasks.

These calculations support the statement that doing the right things is more important than doing things right. The example illustrates how aptly this wisdom applies to the real estate profession. You may write the most eloquent ads, but it's doubtful anyone will pay you $150 an hour for them. Focusing on the big payoff will.

THE LIFE CYCLE OF A REAL ESTATE AGENT

The only constant in real estate, as in most things, is constant change. The market changes: One year, every street in town seems to be lined with "for sale" signs and buyers are few and far between. The next year, buyers seem to arrive by the planeload and there isn't a "for sale" sign to be seen.

Your needs and working habits will also change to meet changing markets as well as to reflect where you are in your professional development and to allow you to make intelligent decisions about where to focus your time and energies.

In time you'll learn other and probably more productive ways to find properties to list than cold-calling. You'll spend more time face-to-face with active buyers and people who are ready to list.

This book is designed to accelerate that change, to hasten your passage through the stages of career development and to achieve what you want to achieve in the shortest possible time. Once you learn to control where and how you spend your time, you will *gain* the time you need to lift yourself into the ranks of agents who devote more of their time to the most rewarding activities. In other words, the better you control your time, the more time you will have to make progress. The process feeds on itself because as you focus on the most rewarding activities, the less rewarding activities that took up much of your day don't even cross your mind.

In a later chapter, you'll calculate the value of your time, which will give you a strong incentive to focus on activities with high rewards. If you then assign value factors to various tasks, you'll have a yardstick by which to measure the value of one activity over another: X dollars an hour for floor time; 1.5X dollars an hour for cold-calling; 2X dollars an hour for working your farm; 3X dollars an hour for showing houses to casual lookers, etc.

You will begin to concentrate on doing the right things, which is more important than doing things right.

CHAPTER 2

Decide What You Want— Today, Next Year, for Life

Since time is all we have, it is the only currency with which to obtain everything else we want. We exchange our time for the rewards we seek from life.

Therefore, the first thing we have to do is decide what we want out of life. What do we want in exchange for our valuable time?

That's a tough question to answer—It requires deep thought. Most people risk missing out on life's greatest pleasures because they never stop to examine where life is taking them and whether that is really where they want to go, be and do. They allow themselves to be carried along by whatever breeze happens to catch their sails. They never learn to control events because they have no sense of direction and no goals. They haven't tried to analyze the value of an activity in terms of time expended versus value received; therefore, any activity is as good as any other. They live for the moment. Only when the ticking of the clock grows too loud to ignore do they ask themselves, "Where am I? Where am I going? Where have I been? What have I accomplished?"

Only after you have examined alternatives and decided what you want from life can you harness your inherent driving force. That driving force is like the sails of a boat. The force varies among individuals, but, large or small, the greatest rewards come to those who hitch their driving force to their examined desires.

Some people travel far and achieve great heights with fairly modest driving force. They discover and exploit vast continents of opportunity, while others, with tremendous energy and power only visit modest islands. Or when they actually stumble onto a continent, they see only the palm trees on the shore before the wind catches their sails and they coast along, missing the gold mines waiting in the interior.

WE NEED TO CONTROL OUR POWER

All the power in the world is of little value if we are unable to steer the boat. Without the ability to hold to a heading, the wind and the tide are in control; events control our lives, instead of the other way around.

Prehistoric people drifted about the face of the earth without apparent purpose until they discovered some means to direct their power. Their initial goals were simple: They were either in pursuit of food or escaping nasty neighbors. They didn't much care where they were going; they just wanted out.

When a group heard that food was abundant and the neighbors friendly in a certain place, they wanted to go *there*. They didn't want to wait for the right wind. They wanted to get moving today and start their new lives tomorrow.

But they still lacked two things: the means to steer and knowledge to steer in the right direction. In other words, they needed a rudder and stars to steer by. But even knowing how to steer isn't enough; we also have to know where we want to go. We need a goal—in fact, we need many goals.

THE POWER OF GOALS

The story is told that the graduating class of a well-known university was asked how many of them had written goals. Only a small percentage had.

Several years later, the same group was asked to report on their financial achievements. The small percentage who had written goals at graduation now accounted for more of the total class wealth than all the other members put together.

A more recent example, cited by Mark Fisher, author of *The Instant Millionaire,* in the June 17, 1990, *New York Times,* concerns a young man working at "a second-rate job in a publishing company." A wealthy publisher wanted to know if he was serious about making money: "How much money do you want to make next year?" he asked.

When the young man gave a vague answer, the publisher handed him a sheet of paper and told him to write down his figure. The publisher then asked why he had set such a low number. He told the young man he could make $20,000 in a month if he set it firmly in his mind as a goal. The young man wrote down the figure and looked at it nightly. At the end of the month, he had made his $20,000 by seizing an unexpected opportunity. He probably would have ignored the opportunity before, but now it conformed to his goal. Today, he is a millionaire.

This is not to suggest that wealth is the only, or even the most important, goal. On the contrary, the whole purpose of time management is to help you pursue all kinds of goals.

For most people, success in their chosen profession is an important goal. As Groucho Marx said, "Money isn't everything, but you'd better have a little." Most of us want more than a little. We want enough to provide a comfortable home and good food for our families, to set aside funds for college educations, to take trips, entertain friends and help worthy causes, to name just a few.

What the examples demonstrate is that goals—written goals—can exert a powerful influence on our behavior. Of course things don't happen just because you write them down; you still have to work at them. The principal purpose of time management is to help you focus on your written goals. Only by focusing your time and energy on your examined goals can you achieve great results.

Goals provide the measuring stick that determines the value of an activity. It forces you to ask some important questions:

- Does this activity support my long-term goals?
- What goal or goals will this assignment help me achieve?
- What can I do with this hour between appointments to further a goal?
- What shall I do tomorrow to move closer to my goals?

Goals help you monitor your activities and your progress. They force you to ask yourself, Is this the best thing for me to be doing right now? What goal am I addressing? Did I get closer to achieving one of

List 2-1

The Things I Want out of Life

my goals today? What should I do tomorrow that will bring me closer to my goals? If you feel yourself drifting aimlessly with the wind, you can trim the sails, lean on the rudder, correct your course and steer for your goal.

If you haven't written down goals for yourself, the best time to start writing them is now. Don't put it off. Set aside a time today to think about goals, and write them down.

Chapter 3 goes more deeply into goals, discussing their various categories and establishing criteria to make them effective. Rather than dive right into goal-setting, let's start by writing down what you want out of life (List 2-1). There's a significant difference: The second option allows, even encourages, you to indulge in the luxury of dreaming—no restrictions. As Bloody Mary sang in *South Pacific,* "You've got to have a dream. If you don't have a dream, how you gonna have a dream come true?" Goal-setting is a more disciplined exercise with stricter rules.

But this is the time and place to dream. Write down 10, 20, even 30 things you want out of life.

When you're finished, we're going to methodically transform those dreams into goals that can be addressed systematically and effectively. If the procedure seems painstakingly slow, remember that goal-setting is the key to success—however *you* define success.

Although practically all books on time management state the importance of goals, few offer any guidelines or procedures for this most important of all exercises. This may be one reason that even though time management has become part of many training programs, the number of people with well-defined and written goals still appears to be very small.

VISUALIZE WHAT YOU WANT YOUR LIFE TO BE ONE YEAR FROM NOW

A mountain climber with artificial limbs was asked what kept him going to reach the top of a high, snow-covered peak.

The weather had been worse than anticipated. Potentially disastrous events hobbled his progress. He had run out of food. He suffered from altitude sickness. Snow blindness added to the danger. His only companion was "Murphy," the one who said that if anything can possibly go wrong, it will.

He answered that he kept imagining himself on top of that mountain, looking back with satisfaction on the difficult climb and the effort he had exerted to reach the heights. Nothing, he said, was going to deprive him of that pleasure.

Nothing did. He derived strength and incentive from his imagination. The mental image of himself on top of the mountain gave him the strength to go on in the face of terrible adversity. He had set his goal and was set on achieving it. He could have said, "Well, nobody told me the weather was going to be this rotten." At the halfway point, he had climbed higher than anyone with artificial limbs ever had. He could have stopped there and said that he'd accomplished more than anyone with his handicaps could ever be expected to achieve. But that would not have satisfied him; that wasn't his goal. His goal was the summit, and by visualizing himself on the summit, he found reserves of strength that enabled him to achieve his goal.

Triathletes, swimmer-cyclist-runners who churn away through 2.4 miles of choppy water, then fight their way through tight clots of speeding bicyclists for another 112 miles before running a full marathon of more than 26 miles, use a similar trick. Asked how they prepare themselves mentally for the ten-hour ordeal, many reply something like, "I'm going to feel so good!" And they believe it. They know that several times, in the course of the race, they'll be in agony. But they imagine the feeling they'll have at the end, the feeling of triumph. Their imagination, the picture of success they carry in their heads, sees them through many hours of peak physical exertion. And their vision of success enables them to achieve it.

Imagining Leads To Achieving

You can use the same technique to help you achieve your goals. Refer back to the list of things you want out of life. We agreed that these were dreams—castles in the air. They lacked the compelling power of goals, because they lacked the essential characteristics of goals, which we will examine in the coming pages.

Let's begin to make those dreams concrete by giving them a time frame. Let's answer the question: What do you want your life to be like one year from today? Do you want to be the top producer in your office? Maybe you want to be the manager. Why not? If you can imagine it, you probably can do it. On the other hand, if you can't picture yourself sitting at the manager's desk, assuming the manager's responsibilities and leading the efforts of the agents in the office, then you probably can't do it—yet. But keep thinking about what a manager has to do and how you would do it. You will begin to create a picture of yourself in the boss's chair.

As your picture of success grows clearer, you will automatically begin to adopt behavior appropriate to the goal you seek.

Role models can be a big help in visualizing what you want to be and have. Who are the people you admire? What do you admire about them? Their ability to penetrate the minds of others and fulfill their dreams? That's an important skill in a real estate person. By observing the behavior of people you admire, you can learn what their skills are and you can begin to adapt them to your personality and situation.

Remember that the people you admire didn't always have the selling and life skills you admire. They probably had to go through a process similar to the one we're describing. They saw people who made them say, "I'd like to be like that," or "I would like to have that person's job, home, leisure time, athletic skills." Note that we are not talking about envy, that most destructive and least productive emotion; we're talking about emulation, which some have called the highest form of flattery. Be that as it may, it is a highly effective technique for getting what you want out of life.

Be Realistic—But Not *Too* Realistic

If you were the smallest kid in your class, your chances of playing varsity football were pretty limited. If you were a girl, you probably had to listen to, "Girls don't play football," until you wanted to scream. But you could be the star of the junior varsity, and the fact is that today girls can and do play football. The luckiest person in the world still has to overcome obstacles. But they can be overcome. One definition of an obstacle is that element that slows other people down as you pass them by.

The proverb that says, "All things come to one who knows how to wait" doesn't explain how to wait. Waiting had better include interim activity, or it could be a very long wait indeed. Passively waiting for something to happen deprives you of the power to make anything happen. Knowing what you want to happen and when you want it to happen are giant steps to making it happen. If you then take constructive action, that's positive and constructive waiting.

Let's say, for example, you have set an income target of $60,000. You're in a location where the average house sale is under $100,000. That means you have to sell or list properties totaling $4 million—40 properties or more, depending on how close to average your sales are. You can wait for the market average to go up, but that's hardly constructive. Or you could work at finding a way to focus on the higher priced properties. If your "farm" is in one of the lower priced areas, you could work at becoming the best "bottom feeder" in the county. The path you take to achieve the success you admire in your role model may differ from his or hers.

The important thing is to create the mental picture of what you want your life to be one year from now. If you're like most real estate people, a year means something in excess of 300 working days and between 2,500 and 3,000 working hours. We'll talk about how to make the most of those hours later; we mention it now to increase your awareness of time. Everything happens in time—things we want and things we don't want. Focusing on the things we do want can help squeeze out the ones we don't. Time, as someone suggested, is what keeps everything from happening at once.

So start creating that picture of yourself leading the life you want to lead in a year. Start with today, so you have a permanent record of the time frame you set for yourself. Remember that you have a date with yourself one year from today when you will have delivered on most, if not all, of those promises you made to yourself. Then look at all the aspects of your life that you want to and can make better—your income, your social life, your athletic skills, your cultural and spiritual opportunities—all the aspects of your life that are important to you.

Part of the goal-setting process is to see where you are now. You know what you're earning, you know where you live, you know what you have in the bank and investments. You know the quality of your social life, your educational achievements, your golf score or your bowling average.

When you have written your description of what your life will be like a year from today, compare the present with the future—the difference between what you have and what you want. That difference defines the "problem."

You want to earn $10,000 a year more than you're earning now? That is a $10,000 problem. You have a three-bedroom house with a living-dining room combination, and you want four bedrooms with a formal dining room? You have a two-room shortfall. You have 86 credits towards a degree that requires 120? The difference between the required number and what you have is the measure of your college-credit problem—a 34-credit problem.

The solution is planning the action that will take you from where you are to where you want to be.

But let's start with that one-year picture. In the previous chapter, we dreamed. Someday, I would like to have, be, see, learn, achieve, go, read or whatever. No deadline, no time frame. Mañana.

But now we need to do something a little different. You're going to paint a picture of the future by describing the life you want to have in one year (List 2–2). Refer back to the "dreams" you wrote down on List 2–1. Select those you want to see come true in the next 12 months.

By creating this portrait, you have taken the first step toward developing a life plan. When you set a deadline for your dreams you have met one of the most important criteria for a goal. By making it part of your one-year picture, you have made it tangible.

List 2-2

Where I Want To Be One Year from Today

Today's date: _____

_____
_____
_____
_____
_____
_____
_____
_____
_____
_____

This portrait will reinforce your desire and help turn your desires into reality. If you remind yourself of the life you expect to be living a year from today, you will adopt the behavior that can make it so. People who think of themselves as managers usually become managers if they do the other things that are part of being a manager. People who think of themselves as effective sales agents usually become effective because they develop the confidence that selling requires.

So keep the picture handy. Look at it from time to time until it becomes part of how you think about yourself—until you are the person in the picture. Like the mountain climber who persisted in imagining himself on top of the mountain until he reached it, the picture you create of yourself will help you realize your desires.

NOW IMAGINE YOUR LIFE IN FIVE YEARS

Now let's get out a more powerful telescope and push that horizon out to five years from now. Five years is a long time. Your children will be five years older; so will you. Your needs will be different, so your priorities will probably have to change.

What do you want your income to be? How much do you want to have invested? In what? You'll probably want to get a leg up on college funds for the children. And it's never too early to start putting something aside for retirement. Few real estate brokerages have retirement plans, so you'd better set aside some funds to supplement Social Security. One thing economists seem to agree on is that anyone planning to live entirely from Social Security payments is planning for a very unpleasant surprise. So get out that pencil and start drawing a picture of where you want to be five years from now.

Let's start with income. Do you want to be making 50 percent more than you figured in your one-year projection? That's about enough to keep up with inflation. One hundred percent more would afford you a somewhat higher standard of living, but not much higher. Maybe you'd better figure on 200 percent to cover your increasing responsibilities, inflation *and* your desire to buy more of life's material pleasures.

You should be thinking about disposable income, i.e., income after taxes. Remember, therefore, that the tax bite will probably be greater. Figure that if you add 10 percent to your annual earnings each year, you'll just about double your income—in unadjusted dollars—every seven years.

Define Your Goals

The main difference between goals and dreams is energy—focused energy. It's easy to dream of a $5,000 bank account; it's just as easy to dream of a $10,000 bank account; or $25,000. You can dream of driving a Rolls-Royce or sailing a 65-foot yacht around the world.

Making the dream come true—achieving the goal—requires that you focus your energy. Before you can start working toward a goal, you have to make it real. You have to believe in it. You have to believe it's something you can and will do. We'll touch on some of the criteria for goals while we work on this five-year picture. We'll refine those criteria in the next chapter when we start to work on lifetime goals.

In addition to being written, a goal must be measurable to be effective. Saying, "I want to be rich" doesn't work. How rich do you want to be? How do you define rich? Some people feel rich when they have some money left over after paying all their bills. Some people feel poor unless they can buy whatever meets their fancy. Remember the example of the young man cited earlier in this chapter. In setting your financial goals, state the dollar amount of the goal: for example, to have $50,000 in liquid assets—bank accounts, stocks, bonds.

Set the Time

By itself, the amount isn't a real goal. You have to set a date to achieve the goal. "Before five years roll by, I will have liquid assets of $_____." Without the date, it's easy to procrastinate. A conversation with yourself might go something like this:

> *You*—Say, weren't you going to have $25,000 or some such sum saved up?
> *The other you*—Yeah, I guess I did. Why?
> *You*—Well, I was just wondering how we're doing.
> *The other you*—We're doing okay.
> *You*—What does that mean?
> *The other you*—It means we've got plenty of time.

At this point, the real you had better step in with something like "No you don't! It's been over a year, and you're no closer today than you were a year ago. Does that mean another year is going to go by without getting one inch closer?" Somebody has to take charge and the only one who can is the real you—the one who sets the goals and the one who can work toward them.

Goal Must Be Realistic

There's one more important test of a goal: It must be realistic and attainable. If it soon becomes apparent that the goal is unattainable, there's a good chance you'll get discouraged. Before that happens, revise the goal in the light of the experience that made you realize the goal was unattainable.

If you are just starting out in real estate, talk to your broker about setting realistic goals. He or she knows the territory and the factors that create the character of the market: average selling price of area homes, number of existing homes coming on the market in an average year, average number of new homes built in the area annually, your company's strength in the market versus the competitive brokers, etc.

On the other hand, don't set a goal that you can attain without serious work. You'll get bored, your mind and your body will go soft and you won't put out the effort that will develop the power and the confidence to tackle greater challenges.

A too-modest goal increases your chance of failure. When Aesop pitted the hare against the turtle, he allowed the hare to believe he would win in a walk. An easy walk. So easy, in fact, he forgot to walk. It was so discouraging that the hare probably retired from racing.

Just as success breeds success, failure breeds failure. It becomes a habit. Whereas success gives you the strength and confidence to tackle the next challenge, failure destroys your confidence. Success tells you you're a winner; failure tells you you're a loser. Set goals you can achieve *with effort,* then make the effort. You'll be a winner.

For these reasons, it is far better to set too ambitious goals than too modest ones. Achieving modest goals doesn't develop muscle. Easy successes lead to complacency. And complacency leads nowhere.

Set ambitious goals, and if they are too big a jump for a day, a week or a month, we'll see about breaking them down into intermediate and short-range goals. The "realistic" criterion can be difficult to determine when you set a five-year goal. But if you translate that five-year goal into a series of one-year goals, each building on the previous year's, you will have done several important things.

First, you will have created a pretty good "reality test." (Is this a realistic objective for this year?) Second, you will have to cut your goal down to a thinkable size. (For many people, the suggestion of being ten years older is unthinkable.) And third, if you take those one-year goals and break them down to six-month goals, and those into one-month goals, you eventually get down to what you have to do each day to reach your goal. Most important, you have converted your five-year goal into a daily action plan.

The point of all this is to encourage you to set ambitious goals. They can be subdued by translating them into shorter-term goals and eventually into daily activities.

That process of breaking down long-term goals is very similar to breaking down large—and even overwhelming—tasks into smaller, quite doable tasks. We'll look further into this when we get into planning in Chapter 6.

Create Your Own Word Picture

A goal isn't really a goal until you've written it down. Use Worksheet 2-1 to create your five-year picture. We've started some of the sentences to make sure that you don't set only financial and career goals. You need a whole set of goals to help you lead a balanced life. Some people try to devote all their time to their careers, and that may seem very commendable at first. But are they really controlling events? Are they enjoying life? Are they contributing to their community? Are they sharing the pleasure and pain of raising children? Are they growing spiritually and intellectually? Are they preserving their health by taking the time to exercise and relax?

If you say that you don't have time for "all those other things," you aren't managing your time. One of the principal aims of time management is to allow time for "all the other things." Time management is based on priorities, and these chapters will help you set priorities, not just to promote your professional interests, but to help you lead a complete life. There are plenty of books about how to succeed. Most of them forget that career success is not all there is to life. Success in one's career is important, but it's only one ingredient in a happy and successful life.

These examples of five-year goals do not begin to exhaust the kinds of goals you can set. In setting goals, you should include all facets of your life—career, family, social, spiritual, educational, physical, recreational, etc.

In later chapters we will allocate time to these activities so that your goals become your guides for living the life you designed for yourself.

As Jane Elizabeth Allen said in *Beyond Time Management* (Addison-Wesley, 1986), goals are like gods. You can't serve them all at the same time, but you ignore individual goals at your peril. Devote too little time to your family, and the day will come when you will ask yourself, "Where was I when the kids were growing up?" It's a terrible question, because you know the answer and there is nothing you can do about it. Skimp on the time you devote to staying healthy, and the day will come when your doctor will say, "You've got to start taking better care of yourself."

The time to think about all those things is now, today, while you're thinking where and what you want to be five, ten, 25 years out. So include all those "gods" in your planning. Serve them well and they will serve you, not only in your real estate career but in your personal life as well.

Worksheet 2-1

My Life in Five Years

Today's date: _____

In five years, my annual earnings will be _____.

My position (title) will be _____.

I expect to be living in _____.
  (city, suburb, street, whatever describes your residential goal)

My home will be worth _____.

I will be driving a _____ (year) _____ (make and model).

My net worth will be _____.

I will have _____ in each child's college fund.

I will spend _____ weeks of uninterrupted vacation with the family.

We will make at least _____ trips together as a family.

I will have dinner with family at least _____ times each month.

I will belong to the following organizations:

_____

_____

_____

_____

_____

I will spend _____ hours each month on community projects or work.

I will have earned _____ continuing education credits to qualify for a management position.

I will read _____ nonbusiness books per month.

Worksheet 2-1 (continued)

> I will weigh _____ pounds.
>
> My waist will be _____ inches.
>
> I will be able to (circle one) swim, run, ski, walk, bicycle, _____ (circle one) miles, meters, yards in _____ (circle one) minutes/hours.
>
> I will take _____ strokes off my golf score.
>
> I will move up _____ "rungs" in (circle one) tennis, racquet ball, squash, handball, _____.

CHAPTER 3

From Dreams to Goals to Action

In the last chapter, we let our imaginations run free and then gradually imposed a few limitations in the form of time frames. We tried to imagine the life we would like to be living at two future points—a year from now and five years from now. We still didn't let reality intrude too harshly—if you can imagine it, you can probably make it happen—while acknowledging that goals must meet certain criteria to be effective guides to our future. We touched on the difference between dreams and goals and reassured ourselves that we can make dreams come true if we are willing to make a *planned effort*.

Before we undertake the arduous task of planning the efforts to attain our goals, let's examine in greater detail the essential requirements goals must meet if they are to do their job of keeping us on track.

ARE THEY YOUR OWN GOALS?

Only you can set goals for yourself. The boss or manager can set quotas—and you have to meet them. But you're the one who has say, "I will sell a million—or two or three million—dollars worth of real estate this year." Salespeople in any field who work only to meet quotas seldom lead the pack. For that reason, some experts feel that quotas are performance-limiters.

"I made my quota" is a defeatist attitude. It says that you let someone else decide what you are capable of doing. Don't let anyone set limits on your performance. You are the best person to decide what you can do. Only you know what reserves of strength and determination you have inside and can call on when you need them.

Leaders come from the ranks of those who set difficult goals for themselves and then make the effort to achieve them, especially when they seem most elusive.

Are Your Goals Challenging?

A goal should require you to stretch. An approach used by many successful agents is to set a goal that seems reasonable and then multiply it by a "stretch factor" of 10, 15 or 20 percent. Your past experience in school, sports, reading or learning a new skill will suggest what it takes to put a burr under your saddle.

If day after day, week after week, you find yourself meeting your goals with ease, set more demanding goals. An athlete who sets a goal of high-jumping six feet doesn't retire when he achieves it. The first time he clears it, he will immediately call to have the bar raised a notch or two. As soon as you achieve a goal, set a new higher one. Records that could "stand forever" are broken every year.

Are Your Goals Measurable?

What are the important dimensions of your goals? How long and how big? Put another way: How much, how many, and when? When you meet a prospect, there are a few things you want to know, such as how big a house they want. How much can they afford to pay? When do they want or need to make a decision?

Make sure you know as much about your goals. How many sales? How many listings? How much money? How many calls? By when? People who don't set dates for achieving goals frequently allow themselves to think, "Oh, there's plenty of time...next month...next year." Days, months, years go by and they are no closer to their goals. Every day should bring you noticeably closer to at least one of your goals. You can't measure your progress if you haven't set a deadline.

Monetary goals can be translated into tasks, and tasks can be translated into hours. If it takes 100 calls to obtain a listing and each call takes an average of five minutes, then you can say that it takes eight hours and 20 minutes to obtain a listing.

If life were that simple, you could sit down at the telephone at 9:00 A.M. and make calls until 5:30 P.M., by which you'd have listed a property. But we all know life isn't that simple. You have to fit your telephone hours around your other activities. With your other duties and responsibilities, it may take a week or more to make those calls. Once you have set the goal and translated it into tasks, you have the incentive to schedule the hours you need to make those calls.

Are Your Goals Realistic?

Some people feel this is the most important requirement of a goal; others say it is the least important. How can you tell if your goal is realistic until you give it your best shot? Can a stutterer become a spellbinding orator? Can a vision-impaired person bowl a perfect game? Can a one-armed man play major league baseball?

Still, if you're a beginner in real estate, you probably shouldn't plan to be the number-one producer in the office—for a while, at least. Some extraordinarily energetic, determined and single-minded people have achieved as much. Most beginners have so much groundwork to do, however, that it may be difficult at first to spend enough time on the activities that result in listings and sales.

As the low person on the totem pole, you may have more floor time than the veterans. You may be assigned open-house duty when you might prefer to be out knocking on doors. You'll be expected to be present for all caravans and attend all meetings.

Working with your broker to establish goals will serve several important purposes. First, you'll get input from an experienced source. Second, you'll know what's expected. Third, you will know that your goals are consistent with company goals and the boss's expectations.

Set Target Dates

We asked the question, "When?" in discussing measurability. We'll ask again now, in an effort to obtain concrete answers and to set definite future dates for achieving goals. A goal without a date is like a check without a signature. It may have some value, but don't try to cash it.

You've heard people talk of long-range goals. They may also speak of immediate goals and intermediate goals, but do all people mean the same thing when they use those subjective terms? For a five-year-old, tomorrow is intolerable, while some mystics visualize a future in eternity. To be practical, setting a long-term goal without a specific date may very well mean "some day."

For instance, you have probably had a would-be buyer say, "We want to move fast on this new home. We've outgrown the house we're in. We're driving each other crazy. And the money is in the bank." Everything points to quick sale.

Six months later, they're still driving each other crazy (and maybe you too) and they're no closer to buying. But they're still in a hurry!

Then again, you may have had the wonderful experience of a caller saying, "I'm coming into town next Tuesday. Here are my wants and price range. I want to see everything you have that fits those parameters, and I expect to make an offer by the end of the day." And does just that!

One thing you'll notice is that the hero of the story (may their kind prosper and multiply!) set a definite time. Our less decisive friend merely said he was in a hurry when he really meant "some day." Yet both would have described their goal of buying a house as short-term, even "urgent."

We'll leave defining the terms *immediate, intermediate* and *long-range* to the semanticists. Like Alice in Wonderland, who said, "I say what I mean.... at least I mean what I say—that's the same thing, you know," people will use words to mean different things. Use the terms *long-term, intermediate* and *short-term* to facilitate reaching your goals, and don't worry about how others use them. Let's instead focus our attention on translating goals into action plans.

In an action plan, you set dates by which you will achieve a certain income, become a manager, earn a degree or move into a new house. The next step is to establish intermediate dates for nearer and nearer dates for reaching certain milestones along the way. Reduce these intermediate dates to still shorter time frames until you come down to what you need to accomplish this month, this week, this day and eventually this hour. Later in this chapter, we will explore the process of translating goals into action.

Are Your Goals Flexible?

Don't let your goals become a straitjacket. They're to help you, not to make your life miserable. What may have been right and true a year ago may not be appropriate today. Your needs and obligations change; so should your goals. They may have been either too ambitious or too modest. Change them. Add to them, but be conscious of what you're doing and why.

What did you have in mind when you set that goal? Did it meet all the criteria for a goal when you set it? What's different today? Don't be discouraged because it's six months since you set that one-year goal, and you're only a third of the way to your goal. Should you change the goal? That's one approach. A better way is to look at what you're doing and see whether you're doing the right things and doing them on time. Few things in life put spring in your step as surely as being on schedule.

If the goal no longer serves your purposes, change it, adjust it or forget it. A goal that isn't consistent with your needs or values is worse than no goal. For example, Charles R. Hobbs in his book *Time Power* advocates starting with unifying principles so that the goals we set are "congruent" with our most cherished values. When we pursue goals that are inconsistent with our values, our lives are not in balance and we experience stress.

Have You Written Them Down?

If you don't write your goals down, they aren't real. They have no power and you will forget or ignore them. Goals are the stars we steer by. Stars aren't useful navigational tools if you can't see them. So it is with goals. They must be visible to remind you constantly of the direction in which you are going.

Have you ever seen a highway sign telling you your destination is 253 miles away? Soon it's 187 miles, then 111, then 58. You're gaining on it when all of a sudden the signs disappear. What happened? Did you miss a turn? Was there a detour? You feel lost and uncomfortable. Out of control. Observing yourself getting closer to a goal is almost as rewarding as reaching it. As you gain confidence, you're encouraged to push on.

Starting with written goals is like knowing your destination when you start a journey. If you refer to them frequently, you will avoid the feeling out of control. Written goals will help you measure your progress and remind you of what you're working for. These reminders are especially important when you are struggling with tasks that are not very rewarding, even though they contribute to the ultimate goal.

Carefully thought-out and written goals help us stay the course by reminding us of the reward we have promised ourselves for all that effort.

Now that we have described the criteria for effective goals, it's time to get on with the business of writing them down. Create the categories you feel contribute to a full and balanced life, such as professional/career goals, financial goals, cultural/intellectual goals or family/marital goals.

GOALS CHANGE WITH TIME

Just as you did when you realized you would not become the astronaut or movie star you dreamed of being when you were in high school, you will find it necessary to reassess your goals as your circumstances and needs change. And that's okay. That's why it's a good idea to allow an entire page, so you can revise, elaborate, delete or add to your goals. Don't feel you have to fill an entire page or that each goal is cast in stone.

What's important is that you write down your goals, review them and your progress regularly and adjust them as a conscious act of control on your part.

The purpose is not to build a narrow one-way path but to create a map and a timetable that will help you address your priorities every day. Very few, if any, maps remain constant, as most Europeans know all too well. But they *are* in some durable form to achieve their purpose, however temporary. So it is with your goals, and they're yours to change when circumstances demand it. By adjusting, refining, polishing and restructuring your goals, you will retain useful and effective tools to keep you headed in the right direction.

At times you will need to change direction or adjust the speed at which you move toward certain goals. You may even have to defer some goals.

As Jane Elizabeth Allen points out, our personal, professional and family goals will sometimes appear to be in conflict. We have to serve these jealous "gods" in turn to keep them all friendly lest they turn on us. How we deal with conflicting goals and priorities is at the heart of time management.

Although writing down goals will not resolve conflicts, it will enable you to recognize when goals appear to be incompatible. Written goals enable you to recognize the conflict, evaluate it, determine which goal must take priority at this time and then take the appropriate action. Sometimes, appropriate action will be to do a Scarlett O'Hara: to say, "I'll think about that tomorrow" and move on. The point is that you have made a conscious decision within the context of all your goals.

Remember, the principal purpose of time management is to put you in control. You aren't in control if you are governed by goals that no longer serve your needs.

Now prepare your own ruled pages as in List 3-1 and start writing. In Chapter 5, we will discuss the importance of using a planner/organizer. Your goals belong on special pages in your planner so that when you plan your day's work, you will have your goals at your fingertips.

TRANSLATE YOUR GOALS INTO ACTION

Back in Chapter 2, you set an income goal as part of your self-portrait one year out. Refer back to that figure and write it on the top line of Worksheet 3-1. Then write down the year in which you will achieve that goal.

The next step is to break down that income goal into a series of shorter term goals. As an example, we'll use a figure of $50,000 to demonstrate the method of reducing that yearly income goal to a useful action guide. It's a nice number, well within the reach of any diligent real estate agent who puts in the effort and uses his or her time to best advantage.

The temptation is to say, "Well, if I break that $50,000 a year down to monthly goals, that's about $4,000 a month. That's my monthly

List 3-1

+-----------------------------------+
| **Professional/Career Goals** |
| |
| _____ |
| _____ |
| _____ |
| _____ |
| _____ |
| _____ |
| _____ |
| _____ |
| _____ |
| _____ |
+-----------------------------------+

goal, and my weekly goal is about $1,000 or about $200 every working day. Let's get going."

But there aren't many $200 days in the real estate business. "Paydays" don't happen every day, and when they do, they come in bigger sizes.

The better way is to convert that one-year money goal into the number of commissions you have to earn on listings and sales to achieve that $50,000 figure. If you work for a multi-city real estate network, you can count on a few referral fees, but they usually don't contribute a large percentage of an agent's income. Besides, your commissions are probably also subject to referral fees, so you'll probably give away as much as you take in in referrals.

What we want to know is how many commissions you have to earn to hit the $50,000 mark. What is the average selling price of homes in your area? Or perhaps a better figure would be the average price of the homes sold by your real estate firm.

Let's take $120,000 as an average sale price. If the commission rate is 6 percent, the average sale nets a $7,200 commission. If this is then

Worksheet 3-1

Income Goal

I will produce a gross income of $_____.

Year in which I will produce that income: _____

---

split 50–50 between the listing and selling broker, each receives $3,600. And assuming the broker splits 50–50 with his or her agents, each sale earns a commission of $1,800 for you as the seller or lister.

If you were both lister and seller, great. But let's look at it as two separate commissions, since each involves separate and quite different activities.

We'll add some lines to the worksheet we started on the previous page to continue the calculation (Worksheet 3-2). And we'll leave the lines blank so you can write in figures that reflect the actual situation and practices in your area and brokerage.

For the sake of the $50,000 example, we'll assume that selling and listing broker do split 50–50 and then split 50–50 with their agents. That makes the average commission to you as the selling or listing agent $1,800. So we divide our $50,000 income target by $1,800 and come up with a performance target of about 28 commissions.

Again, let's resist the temptation to spread those 28 commissions over a working year. Instead, let's convert those 28 commissions to the activities that produce commissions—showing properties to people who are (1) interested in buying and are capable of buying or (2) talking to people who have properties to list and are motivated to sell.

It's an old adage that in real estate "listing is the name of the game." Maybe so. But the funny thing is that for every seller, there has to be a buyer. In the long run, there will be as many listing commissions as there are selling commissions. You may work your territory so effectively that you list ten houses in a month or three months. But there's no commission until there's a sale. Also, a stellar listing period may reflect a decline in the desirability of the area and a correspondingly higher sales resistance.

That said, it's true that some people are more effective in obtaining listings than in matching up buyers with available properties. There-

Worksheet 3-2

Income/Commission Goal

I will produce a gross income of $_____.

Year in which I will produce that income: _____

Average sale in my area and brokerage $_____

Standard commission percentage _____%

Average gross commission per sale $_____

Percentage to selling broker _____%

Percentage to listing broker _____%

Selling broker's commission $_____

Listing broker's commission $_____

Percentage of listing commission to me _____%

Percentage of selling commission to me _____%

Actual listing commission to me $_____

Actual selling commission to me $_____

---

fore, feel free to divide those requisite 28 commissions in any way that best reflects your talents and experience.

Generating commissions calls for action, so let's take the next step and plan those actions (Worksheet 3-3).

Notice that we eliminated some of the middle lines, but kept the top line—the income line—in place, just to keep that written goal in front of you.

To complete the process, calculate the actions that will produce the number of listings you have targeted. And do the same for selling properties. We used the rule of thumb that it takes 100 calls to produce one listing. Your experience may be different, but whatever it tells you, convert that number of listings into the number of calls that will produce them.

Worksheet 3-3

> **Agent's Income/Commission Goal**
>
> I will produce a gross income of $_____.
>
> Year in which I will produce that income: _____
>
> Average *agent's* commission in my brokerage $_____.
>
> Total number of commissions required to meet my gross income target _____.
>
> Number of listing commissions I will earn: _____
>
> Number of selling commissions I will earn: _____

Let's divide the total number of commissions in our example by two and set 14 listing commissions and 14 selling commissions as the target. Then, using the "100" rule, we need to make 1,400 calls to produce 14 listings. That comes out to a little fewer than 30 calls per week. That's your action target to secure the listings that you calculated in Worksheet 3-3.

Those calls are what you now must extend over the one year. That will be part of the planning process described in Chapter 6.

The intensity of activity required to produce 14 selling commissions can be calculated in similar fashion, although not quite as simply. What does your experience, or that of others in your office, suggest? How many properties do you have to show to how many prospects to make a sale? Some people look at three houses in one morning and make an acceptable offer the same day with closing scheduled in six weeks. Others want to look and look and look. And then again, some agents convert lookers to sellers with greater ease—and in less time— than others.

Therefore, there is no easily derived equation, but you can set targets for the number of prospects you will show properties to, translate that into a per-month figure and evaluate your results. If you hit your target, make next month's a little more challenging. If you fall short, try to schedule more face-to-face meetings with prospective buyers.

Adjust Listing and Selling Activities

Analyze the activities that produce sales, and you may find that the ratio of "B" time (supporting action) to "A" time (face-to-face) is much higher in selling than in listing. You have less control over face-to-face time with buyers than with sellers. If you don't have a long list of prospective buyers you're taking around, your most rewarding activity will probably be to serve your listings.

Those activities vary with market conditions. An economic growth area probably attracts many newcomers. If large companies are bringing people in, the personnel department may offer assistance in finding homes. If the director knows you and your company, he or she may refer people.

The need is to identify the activities and schedule them so you retain control. Design a program that focuses your time and energy on predetermined action based on your analysis of what conditions call for.

Aggressive salespeople say that a tough market is a seller's market, turning the common wisdom on its head. Their point is that when the market is slow, the salesperson who gets out and roots—the "sellers"—are the winners. You can root desperately, or you can root smart. Which brings us back to working smarter—in this case, smarter than the next person.

You accomplish this by scheduling the activities you have determined will produce the desired results. You may have to revise your assumptions regarding listing versus selling. If you have five or ten listings that aren't moving, is it wise to devote much time to securing more listings? The name of the game is really *commissions*. The role of time management is to encourage you to analyze what produces commissions under existing conditions. And making sure that those activities are where you invest your time.

CHAPTER 4

Define Your Responsibilities

The last chapter dealt with goals—your goals. But as John Donne said a long time ago, "No man is an island." Your goals affect others, just as their goals affect you. More to the point, no one ever achieved very much without the support of others. Similarly, we have responsibilities for and obligations to others at work, at home, in our community.

So before we get so completely absorbed in the details of our own life and our own goals, let's take a look at those others on whom we rely to reach our goals and who can help us achieve a complete and balanced life.

The best way to do this is to list the people and institutions that depend on you and that you depend on. We'll suggest a few categories and leave room for you to add those that make your life unique.

THE WORKPLACE

Let's start here, since work probably takes up the biggest chunk of your time. We'll defer the various *task* responsibilities and consider first the *people* responsibilities. Divide the list into two categories: those who depend on you and those you depend on (List 4-1). Under the name, state briefly what those responsibilities are—what is expected of you and what others expect of you.

List 4-1

People Responsibilities	
I depend on:	**These depend on me:**
_____	_____
_____	_____
_____	_____
_____	_____
_____	_____
_____	_____
_____	_____
_____	_____
_____	_____
_____	_____

If more than ten people depend on you and vice versa, use an additional piece of paper. Or you might want to consider how to reduce the number! You may be pulled in too many directions; trying to keep too many people happy can consume a lot of time and increase stress.

FAMILY

The other "most important" obligation the majority of people have is to their families. Here your responsibilities are both easier and more difficult to define. Your boss can usually tell you precisely what is expected of you. Family responsibilities, however, usually require a good deal of negotiation with your spouse and children.

There are many books on how to manage a stressless home. The point they have in common is that every family member should take on clearly defined responsibilities. You and your spouse can start by listing things that need to be done in the home, such as cooking, cleaning, shopping, dishes, gardening, feeding pets and so on. Once all parties

List 4-2

Responsibilities to My Family	hours/week

agree on what has to be done to keep the home running, assignments are made on the basis of time required, age, skills, and responsibilities away from the home, such as earning a living. Homework, after-school job, PTA, etc., all need to be considered in this exercise.

Since this is your list, only write down the home responsibilities that you take on (List 4-2). A useful wrinkle at this point is to include an estimate of the time required to fulfill each of them. The importance of this step will become apparent when we get into time analysis in Chapter 8.

COMMUNITY

Most people have many obligations in addition to their jobs and their families. Some people make serious commitments to organizations such as the Lions, Kiwanis, Optimists, Rotary and so on. Others are deeply involved in work for their religious institutions. Still others are intensely loyal to and work for the good of their alma mater.

List 4-3

My Civic, Religious, School, Etc. Responsibilities	hours/week

Give these interests the importance they deserve and make them a part of your life plan. Remember that the aim of time management is to help you build a balanced life, not necessarily to make you the most successful real estate agent in town. Figure out how much time you can or want to devote to these activities (List 4-3). Then when we get into the business of scheduling, you'll know how much time to allocate, and the all-important *when*.

You now have your "job description." It's different from the usual job description in that it reflects the kind of life you have chosen for yourself, not the kind of life that many people are forced into because they have not learned to control events.

Taking the time to create such an inventory of obligations gives you power to make a conscious decision about what is important. It reduces the number of surprises and emergencies that disrupt so many people's plans. You have taken an important step in writing your own "marching orders."

Define Your Responsibilities

ALLOCATE TIME TO EACH AREA OF RESPONSIBILITY

Now that you have inventoried your responsibilities, you are in a position to think about how much time to allocate to each. You have already made preliminary time allocations for some areas. Without such allocations, you risk losing control—you will have no reliable mechanism to sound an alarm when one responsibility takes up too much time.

Again, work is a good place to start. How many hours a week are you going to work? The average full-time real estate person works 50 hours a week. Some work many more. It's a question you must answer for yourself, probably after a serious discussion with your boss. Following is a list of typical real estate tasks. For now, you need only make a tentative commitment to the number of hours you're going to work, leaving enough time for the other obligations you list.

_____ Telephoning for appointments with potential listers

_____ Making personal calls in your "farm" area

_____ Compiling listings for prospective buyers

_____ Talking with potential listers

_____ Working caravans

_____ Sitting open houses

_____ Showing houses to prospective buyers

_____ Scanning the multilist book or computer

_____ Working phone duty at the office

_____ Typing up offers

_____ Attending closings

_____ Presenting and negotiating offers

_____ Attending meetings

_____ Training new associates

_____ Mailing cards and other reminders to prospects

_____ Preparing advertisements to promote listings

_____ Obtaining appraisals

_____ Previewing homes

_____ Messengering

_____ Arranging for inspections

_____ Calling attorneys

_____ Calling banks and other lenders

_____ Calling on buyers' new neighbors

_____ Qualifying buyers

_____ Attending planning boards for leads on new tracts

_____ Taking real estate courses

_____ Obtaining certificates of occupancy

_____ _____

_____ _____

_____ _____

This is a fair overview of the tasks most real estate agents must perform, although the list will vary with geographical locations and brokers. This is why we have provided a few blank lines so you can write in any tasks that have been omitted.

Classify the Tasks

Now go back over the checklist above and, using the categories described earlier, assign the appropriate letter to each task. To review:

- *A* refers to being face-to-face with a prospect. That is the only kind of activity that can generate a commission and produce income.
- *B* is for activities that prepare you for *A* activities, such as compiling a list of possible houses and making appointments.
- *C* is for real estate activities that are not directly related to selling, such as putting up signs, messengering and writing reports.

Define Your Responsibilities

In the open space before each task description, insert A, B, or C to indicate the value of the activity.

We did not include activities that do not relate to real estate. The reason is that we need to make a conscious decision regarding how we apportion our time between work and leisure. How many hours a week do you want to spend on your job? Again, you need to make this decision after consulting with your boss or manager.

Once you decide, you have some means of protecting your nonwork time. Strive to abide by your decision, allocating work time to A, B and C activities according to their income-producing potential, but not exceeding your total work-time commitment. It is the surest means to achieving all the goals you set—and not letting your career absorb all your time. It helps you maintain the balance you were seeking when you set goals for every aspect of your life.

Based on your priorities, you may have to alter the preliminary time calculations you've made. The critical decision you have to make at this point is what *percentage* of your time you are going to devote to each activity? Some will be easy because they are part of the office routine. You probably have a weekly sales meeting. You may be told how many hours to sit open houses. Desk time may also be prescribed by the boss. So you know how many hours each of those activities will occupy on a weekly basis.

Write down the hours per week for each of these "command performance" activities. The total is your nondiscretionary work time. It's required of you, and there's very little you can do about it, even though none of those activities will produce income.

Say it adds up to 22 hours a week, and that you've decided you're going to work an average of 50 hours a week. That leaves you 28 hours of discretionary work time, time you can spend as you want—mainly doing the things that will generate commissions or prepare you for face-to-face meetings with prospects.

Now make a preliminary allocation of those 28 hours over the other activities—principally A and B activities.

How much time can you reasonably expect to spend on A activities, when you're face-to-face with someone who can make a buying or listing decision? Some agents feel they're doing well if they manage 5 percent—less than three hours a week. Others expect to be in a selling or listing mode 25 percent of the time.

If you're new, you'll have to assign a lot of time to prospecting. We'd all like to spend all of our time listing or showing, but that isn't likely. On the other hand, you know you *have* to spend a certain amount of time listing and selling to meet your income goal.

So make some tentative time allocations for each activity, try it for a month, and then take a reading. You'll see whether you're spending too much time preparing and not enough face-to-face. Your time log (Chapter 7) will show how you're using your time. Later in that chapter, you will analyze your performance over a second period of time, as you make a conscious effort to stick to your guidelines.

You will be able to see where to make adjustments and reapportion the time you've devoted to those activities. Or you may find you have to re-evaluate your total time commitment to meet your income goals. If you're not spending enough face-to-face time and you can't reduce preparation and nondiscretionary time, that may be the unhappy answer.

Don't despair. Rewards in the real estate business are usually cumulative. The groundwork you lay today may bring rewards well into the future. You'll probably find that as your reputation grows, you will secure listings with a smaller time investment. People will call you because of the track record of fast sales you have created.

The other good news is that as you reap the results of increased face-to-face time, your nondiscretionary time will become more productive, because you'll become more adept at applying information gathered during those activities to your selling and listing efforts. You'll learn to use desk time to your advantage. Your growing success may even entitle you to miss meetings and caravans in favor of income-producing activities. You'll be able to cash in on past favors and ask another agent to stand in for you at an open house. The important thing here is to make tentative commitments to spend a predetermined share of your time on the various parts of your job.

WHAT DO YOU HAVE TO DO?

Did you ever wake up in the middle of the night and feel overwhelmed by the number of things you have to do: the signs to put up, the calls to make, the hedge to trim, the letters to answer, the ads to write and on and on? You don't know where to begin.

Here's a suggestion. Start making a list. If it's the middle of the night (that's when that kind of terror often strikes), and you can't get back to sleep because of the pressure you're feeling, that's a good time to start. Get up, go to your desk and start listing your tormentors.

Two things will happen. First, you'll get some relief from writing the list. Disorganized as it will be at the outset, it will help you identify the myriad tasks that are chasing each other around in your head. Second, your list is a tangible and powerful weapon to help you tame that unruly mob of tasks and get them into line.

When you've written down all you can think of, put down the pencil, turn off the light and go back to bed. You still may not have any idea how you're going to get all those things done, but at least you have a handle on *what* you have to do. Making the list has a cathartic value, like a good cry or a scream. It gets things off your chest.

Of course, you may wake up tomorrow night with a few more tasks you hadn't thought of the first time around. Add them to your list. Corral all those undone tasks in one list. If you're in the habit of jotting things down on paper napkins or the backs of envelopes, transfer everything to one list.

But don't let list-making become an occupation in itself. There's a technique known as the "mind dump," in which you just keep writing until you've listed every possible thing that you can think of, now and in the future. The danger of this is that you spend too much time listing the things you have to do, leaving little time to hack away at the list. Some people spend so much time talking about what they're going to do that they don't get around to doing much of anything.

So, before you list all the things you're going to do in the next 20 years, go back and decide what needs to be done first. Some items may require immediate attention. Get them out of the way first so you can concentrate on the most important things on your list.

Important versus Urgent

Notice we said *important*. That's very different from *urgent*, but many people have a hard time recognizing the difference and disciplining themselves to tackle important things and let the merely urgent take care of themselves.

Look at it this way: When the baby cries in the middle of the night, that's *urgent*. At least, that's what the baby is trying to tell you. If he or she can persuade you of the urgency, you'll get up, warm the bottle, change the diaper, sing a little song, whatever is necessary to stop the crying so you can get back to sleep.

On the other hand, saving for the baby's education is *important*. That too can awake you with a jolt in the middle of the night if "baby" has been admitted to a pricey college, and you haven't the foggiest idea how you're going to pay for it. But it illustrates the difference. *Urgent* is usually short-term; immediate resolution of an unexpected problem is called for. *Important* usually involves intermediate or long-range goals.

Time management and its indispensable companion, planning, provide the means to complete important tasks before they become urgent. Urgent tasks keep you from tackling the truly important ones. Sometimes they provide an excuse for avoiding difficult but important tasks.

If you live in the Snow Belt, you've checked your anti-freeze long before the weather prophets announce a deep freeze and you have to scramble to find an open service station. If you live in Georgia, don't wait until August to check your car's air-conditioning. It will become urgent some day in July when you risk boiling a customer. Both of these are important tasks, that, if ignored, can quickly become urgent ones.

Our attitude toward the telephone provides another example of the difference between important and urgent and our inability to recognize and act on the difference. Most people are utterly incapable of ignoring a ringing telephone. We always treat the telephone as if we were expecting a call from the White House.

Even the answering machine has done little to reduce the phone's tyranny; we still race to answer it. Maybe the person won't leave a message; maybe they won't call back. If it's important, they will leave a message or call back.

Peter Drucker, a management consultant who understands the importance of time, said doing the right things is more important than doing things right. We spend too much time perfecting the trivial and too little time identifying and tackling the tasks directly related to achieving goals. I once had a boss who spent the first three months in her new job working on her business card. It was the most carefully designed business card in the organization. She was gone before she had a chance to accomplish much else.

We spend too much time racing for the telephone instead of focusing on the activities that can generate commissions. Because the telephone can be a major distraction, we'll look at ways to control it in Chapter 8.

This is not to say that some urgent tasks cannot also be important. Rescuing a drowning person is both urgent and important. Keeping an appointment with a prospective lister is important. And if five minutes before the appointment, you're ten miles away, it's urgent.

Knowing the outstanding features of the house you intend to show is important; being ready for your client is important. The urgency of these tasks will depend on how well you've planned. Planning is the art of avoiding urgency, which we will deal with in future chapters.

Get the Priorities Straight

A problem with the "mind dump," listing every possible thing you can think of, is that you list tasks in the order in which they come to your mind. Which probably means all the "urgent" tasks are at the top of the list. Some truly important tasks—those most likely to relate to long-range goals—may appear at the bottom of the list. There are too many crying babies in a mind dump, and not enough saving for a college education.

Don't work off your raw list. You have to massage it into a useful guide to your daily, weekly and monthly activities.

Earlier in this book, we assigned the highest priority to face-to-face activities because they are directly related to generating commissions. We assigned the second level of priority to activities that prepare us for or lead us to face-to-face meetings. We reserved the third level for real estate-related activities that don't involve or lead to face-to-face opportunities. These tasks are an unavoidable part of the business. And though we assigned them the lowest priority, we recognize that they must be done.

We can now apply the same criteria to our list of tormenting tasks. The first step is to separate your list into real estate activities—business-related activities—and activities not related to real estate. Set the latter aside for now.

Quickly go through the real estate list and break it up into the three categories. Now you have three lists: activities that are important because they can generate commissions; activities that can prepare you for or lead you to commissions; and finally obligatory tasks that are unrelated to producing commissions.

The next step is to look at the *A* list and organize its elements in order of importance. They're all important because they rated an A, but some are more important than others. This is where urgency may rear its head. If there's an important item—an opportunity that won't last, a hot prospect arriving in town next week—make that your A-1. That's the task you will work on first thing in the morning—and work on it until it is complete. It's the task you will enter in your planner (Chapter 6) during your daily planning session.

You'll notice that "working on that task until it's complete" means any other urgent tasks have to wait. You can't have two A-1s. Decide ruthlessly which is more important. Ruthlessly, because you will decide on the basis of which best serves your interests.

If they are equally important and urgent, you may have to analyze each task as urgent or not-so-urgent. This will enable you to attend to the truly urgent and defer action on the less urgent, thus keeping all the balls in the air and amazing everyone with your ability to deal with all kinds of pressure.

Is It Really That Easy?

We glossed over a few major points in the urgent-important discussion, suggesting that the distinction is always easy to make. It isn't; nor is it always easy to act on the distinction even when it's clear.

If an unforeseen event threatens a deal, that's urgent. You do what you have to to save it. You may have to defer an important task. That's pretty straightforward.

But real estate work and transactions are always composed of multiple tasks. Wouldn't it be great if you could sit down at your desk and work at the task until it's complete? It might be, but it wouldn't be real estate. We're not building a dog house because Fluffy is pregnant. We're usually putting together a complex transaction involving at least a dozen people, very few of whom dance to the same tune.

Furthermore, we're apt to be working on two, five, ten or even twenty deals at any given time. And they're all important. However, not every task that must be completed before closing becomes urgent at the same time. There are long periods of waiting: waiting for the counteroffer, waiting for the counteroffer to be countered, waiting for the title search.

What you have is a queuing problem: getting all those events to form an orderly and manageable line so you can attend to each one in time and never allow an urgency to develop. Urgencies bring ants to the picnic, and we know that urgencies will occur, despite our best efforts. We'll go into greater detail on queuing and ways to organize action in Chapter 6.

The next chapter will show you how to put together a system that will, first, help you stick to your commitments, and second, provide you with an accurate record of how you spend your time over an extended period. If that record shows that you are not spending your time doing the right things, you'll have the knowledge you need to make appropriate adjustments to achieve your predetermined goals.

CHAPTER 5

Create a System

We have created a number of lists—of goals, obligations, responsibilities, things to do. We've analyzed the job in terms of component tasks and made tentative commitments as to time—both total time and time allocated to various components. These were preliminary and necessary exercises, which will lead to your gaining control over events.

We now need to consolidate those lists into a program of action—a plan. The plan will help you focus on your priorities and work toward your professional and career goals, while still leaving time for activities that contribute to a full and balanced life.

Although it is true that time is money, the fact remains that most of us are obligated to spend time doing things that have little to do with making money.

Although these low-priority activities may appear to have little bearing on goals, they have a lot to do with running a real estate business—keeping the boss happy, to which we need to assign a high priority. If the boss says everyone must attend a three-hour meeting every Monday morning, everyone had better show up. Once you calculate the value of your time (Chapter 9), you can figure what the meeting costs you. Multiply that by the number of your colleagues who attend and you may be able to negotiate your way out of it on occasion, but that is another subject for another time.

For now, let's concentrate on creating a system that will pull all our goals, commitments and obligations together so we can address and execute them in an orderly fashion. We'll call the system a planner, because that is its ultimate purpose.

EVERYTHING IN ONE PLACE

Everyone in real estate has an appointment book. But an appointment book isn't enough to allow you to control events.

Although you have some freedom in setting the time for appointments, they are essentially nondiscretionary ones. Once made, they are usually obligatory. Our goal here is to control discretionary time. When you fill an hour of discretionary time with an appointment, you convert it to nondiscretionary time.

For the sake of this discussion, let's define discretionary time as time between appointments and other obligations. Your success and your earnings will depend to a large extent on how well you use that discretionary time to work on your goals and priorities. To do that requires a means to schedule appointments that is not only reliable and positive, but that also opens up time to work on projects and develop opportunities that will advance your professional and personal goals.

For lack of a better term, let's call it a time management system. You can also call it a personal productivity system or a personal management system. The last term comes closest, because as we tried to show earlier, you can't really manage time. You can manage how you spend your time, and you must manage yourself and how you use the time available.

Whatever you call it, your system should serve five essential functions:

1. Appointment calendar. You live by appointments—with prospective buyers and listers, mortgage lenders, lawyers, etc. You have to *be* there.
2. Time log. To control your time, you need to know how you spend your time. This will provide you with visible evidence of how successful you were in using your time to achieve your goals. Evaluating this record of how you spent your time will help you increase your personal productivity.
3. "Things to do" list. During your daily planning session (which we will discuss further in Chapter 6), you will write down the things

you need to do that day, or the next day, if you do your planning in the evening. Your system then ensures that you tackle the most important items first. At first, you may work off the master list of things to do that you created with your "mind dump."
4. Tickler-reminder. Your system should provide the means to plan and schedule the steps you must take on the way to achieving your goals. This is more than slotting an appointment for two weeks down the road. It's a reminder to work on a certain project at a certain time so that you stay on schedule. It's also a means to schedule the components of tasks that stretch over a period of time.
5. Expense record. You need to keep an accurate record of all your business-related expenses for income-tax and reimbursement purposes. Your system should provide a convenient way to accurately record expenses as they are incurred.

Stationers and direct marketers sell a wide variety of planning systems. They vary from appointment books with a few blank pages for notes to costly leather binders you can stuff with information on everything from the exchange rate in Malacca to the mean temperature in Reykjavik.

Because I am most familiar with the Day-Timers™ system and have used it for a number of years, the illustrations in this book are of Day-Timers pages. The system is available in a range of formats, page sizes and special insert pages to suit individual needs. One of this system's principal advantages is that you can start with a fairly simple system and elaborate on it as you become more familiar with it, more conscious of your actual needs and more skilled in planning your work.

Don't start with a complicated system that takes more time and effort than it saves. You'll quickly tire of it and cast it aside. Much better to start with one that meets the five basic requirements, get used to it and then add optional pages as you see the need for them.

The format we'll use here is the two-page-per-day reference format in the junior desk size (Figures 5-1 and 5-2). This format is well suited to the needs of most real estate people. It isn't so bulky that you'll grow tired of carrying it, yet it provides enough space to accommodate the needs of all but the busiest salesperson.

Also, it recognizes that real estate people don't work an eight-hour day or a five-day week. The "appointments and scheduled events"

Figure 5-1. Left-hand page of a typical two-page-per-day planner.

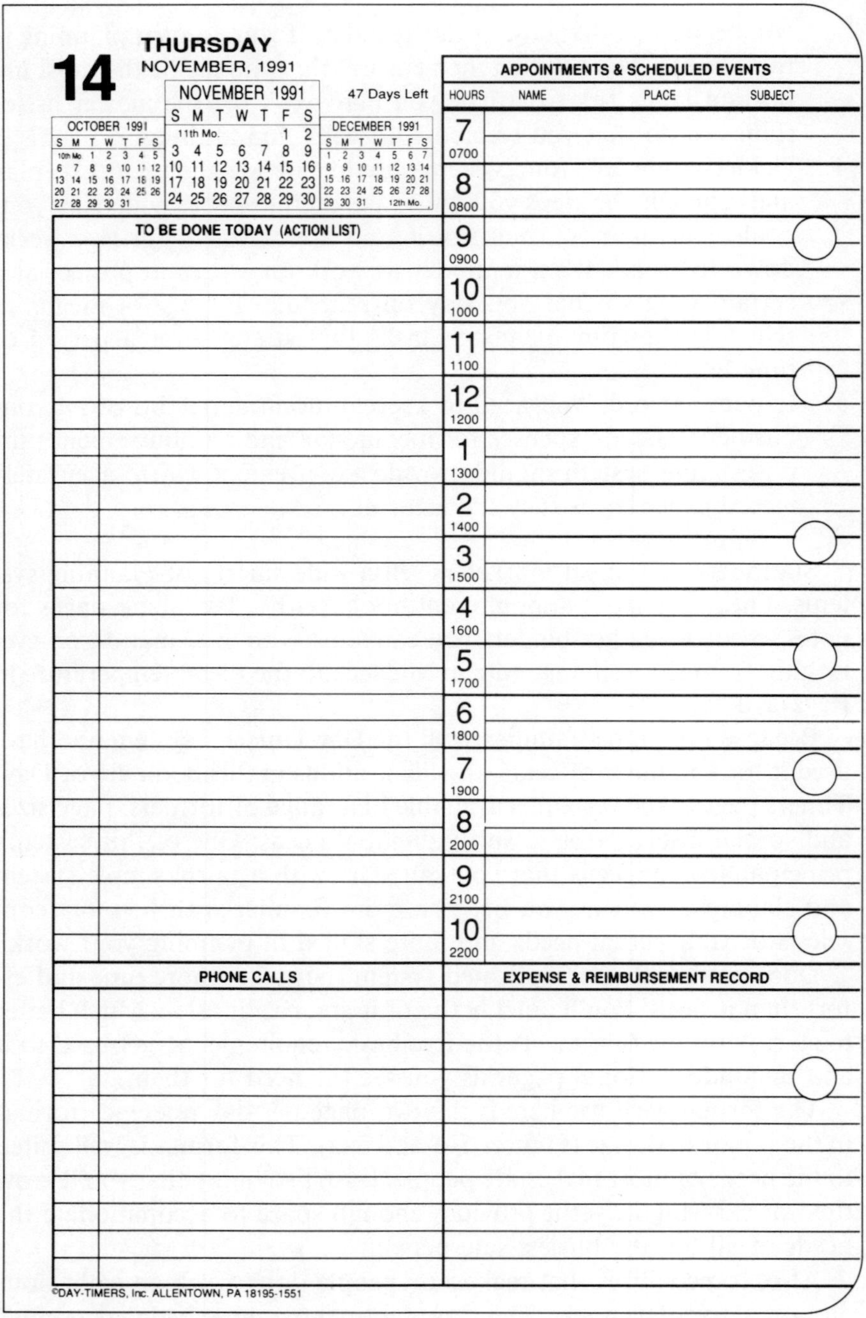
14 **THURSDAY**
NOVEMBER, 1991

47 Days Left

OCTOBER 1991						
S	M	T	W	T	F	S
10th Mo.		1	2	3	4	5
6	7	8	9	10	11	12
13	14	15	16	17	18	19
20	21	22	23	24	25	26
27	28	29	30	31		

NOVEMBER 1991						
S	M	T	W	T	F	S
11th Mo.					1	2
3	4	5	6	7	8	9
10	11	12	13	14	15	16
17	18	19	20	21	22	23
24	25	26	27	28	29	30

DECEMBER 1991						
S	M	T	W	T	F	S
1	2	3	4	5	6	7
8	9	10	11	12	13	14
15	16	17	18	19	20	21
22	23	24	25	26	27	28
29	30	31		12th Mo.		

TO BE DONE TODAY (ACTION LIST)

APPOINTMENTS & SCHEDULED EVENTS

HOURS	NAME	PLACE	SUBJECT
7 0700			
8 0800			
9 0900			
10 1000			
11 1100			
12 1200			
1 1300			
2 1400			
3 1500			
4 1600			
5 1700			
6 1800			
7 1900			
8 2000			
9 2100			
10 2200			

PHONE CALLS

EXPENSE & REIMBURSEMENT RECORD

©DAY-TIMERS, Inc. ALLENTOWN, PA 18195-1551

Illustration courtesy of Day-Timers™, Inc.

Figure 5-2. Right-hand page of two-page-per-day planner, which serves as both time log and diary.

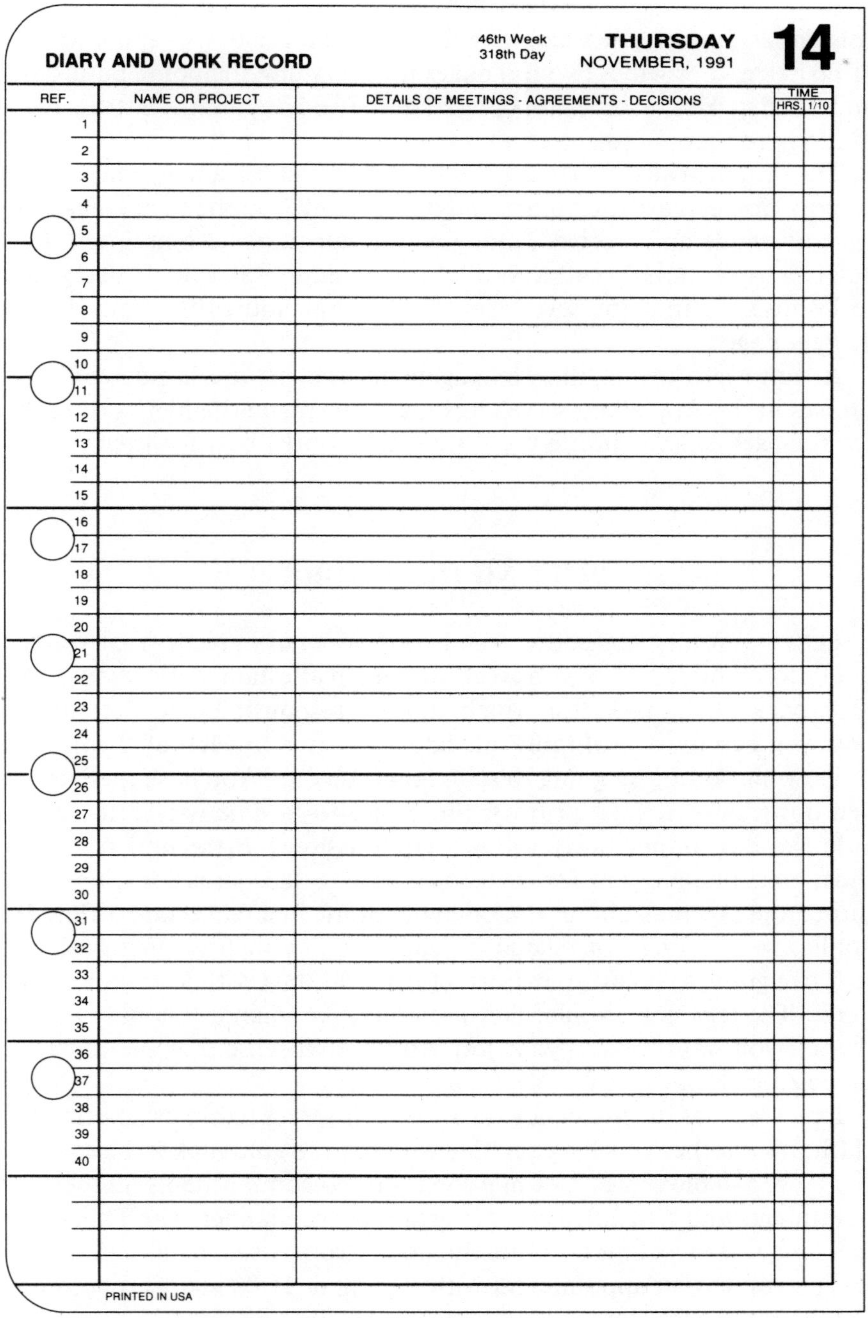

Illustration courtesy of Day-Timers™, Inc.

column allows for a working day that begins at 7:00 A.M. and ends at 11:00 P.M. and provides two full pages for every day, including Saturday and Sunday. You're under no obligation to use every line of every page, but they're there if you need them.

The "phone calls" block is probably too small for a busy real estate person. You can use the "diary and work record" on the facing page to list calls made and received, along with other tasks accomplished. Or you can use optional "call record" pages (Figure 5-3) that are designed to be inserted into the seven-ring binder that houses the daily Day-Timers pages.

A number of other time management systems are listed with addresses in the Appendix, so readers may investigate the merits of each for themselves and choose the system that works best for them.

PUTTING IT TO WORK

Let's say you have decided—and your boss has agreed—that you're going to commit 50 hours a week to your real estate work. Now let's look back at the tasks for which you are responsible and determine how you can most profitably allocate your time to each of them.

How much are you going to spend on each one? You have them broken down into A, high priority, those face-to-face activities that provide the best opportunity to earn commissions; B, second priority, those that prepare you for or lead to face-to-face situations; and C, those housekeeping chores that are part of life in a real estate office. D applies to activities not related to real estate, so we'll set them aside.

We're going to break an important rule and start with lowest priority items. The reason is simple: they are nondiscretionary. You have to do them if you want to keep your job. And in that sense they become the highest priority.

Don't let that inconsistency throw you. It serves to illustrate priority clash; it's another corollary on "He who has the gold makes the rules."

Figure 5-4 illustrates how one agent slotted commitments on the appointments and scheduled events portion of the planner. The Thursday morning sales meeting occupies the hours from 8 A.M. to 10 A.M. Then this person has an appointment with a client at 11:00 A.M. and nothing for the rest of the day.

Figure 5–3. Supplementary call record sheet on which to either schedule or record phone calls.

CALL RECORD

Company ____________________

Address ____________________

City, State, Zip ____________________ Phone ____________________

Contacts ____________________

Date of Call	✔	No.	Details of Call (Number Each Item)	Due Date

DAY-TIMERS RE-ORDER No. 90678 — Printed in USA

✔ When Completed

Illustration courtesy of Day-Timers^{TM}, Inc.

Figure 5-4. Day-Timers™ page with appointments and scheduled activities filled in.

THURSDAY NOVEMBER 14, 1991		
TO BE DONE TODAY (ACTION LIST)	**HOURS**	**APPOINTMENTS & SCHEDULED EVENTS** (NAME / PLACE / SUBJECT)
1 Make 10 phone calls (see call record)	7 0700	
2 Send cards to all Allens' neighbors	8 0800	Sales Meeting
3 Gift for Dot	9 0900	↓
4 Read next chapt of R.E. Practice	10 1000	
5 Get car washed	11 1100	Meet Landons at 109 State
	12 1200	
	1 1300	
	2 1400	
	3 1500	
	4 1600	
	5 1700	Shop for gift
	6 1800	
	7 1900	
	8 2000	
	9 2100	
	10 2200	
PHONE CALLS		**EXPENSE & REIMBURSEMENT RECORD**

Illustration courtesy of Day-Timers™, Inc.

Hint: If your sales meetings frequently run overtime, a good strategy is to schedule a meeting with a prospect as close to the scheduled end of the sales meeting as practical—leaving time to get to the place where you are meeting the prospect. The main benefit is that you create a tight schedule that reduces the temptation to fritter away that hour.

Another important benefit is that you have an excellent reason to leave the meeting if it runs over. That simple strategy restores priorities to their proper rank: You've left a C activity for a A activity—a face-to-face meeting with a prospect.

But let's assume that your appointment with your prospect was for 11:00 A.M. You may have an hour between the meeting and your appointment. Or you may not, if the meeting runs over. In making your daily plan, you need to build in some flexibility. You can't count on squeezing a full hour's work into that hour, because you might not have an hour. But do plan to use it constructively.

How about phone calls? One way to increase efficiency in use of time is to group similar activities and perform them in a single block. Telephone calls are perfect candidates for filling in short time slots. So look at your to do list during your daily planning session, pick out the most important telephone calls, and schedule them for that hour.

Now where do you have to be for that 11:00 A.M. appointment? Over near the Murtagh development. What do you have going over there? What *should* you have going over there? Obviously, if the Murtagh development is in your territory, you should take the opportunity to investigate, make yourself known or follow up previous contacts while you're in the neighborhood. After the telephone, the biggest thief of your discretionary time is unnecessary travel.

But both the telephone and unnecessary travel will continue to rob you unless you take steps to prevent them. The time to take those steps is during your daily planning session (Chapter 6).

CHAPTER 6

Plan Each Day's Activities, But Expect the Unexpected

Let's examine a little more closely the concept of discretionary and nondiscretionary time so you can define them more precisely and relate them to your daily plan.

As we mentioned earlier, nondiscretionary time is time taken up by "command performances." The weekly meeting, desk time and sitting open houses are command performances; you're told where to be, at what time, what's expected of you and when you're free to leave. What's left is discretionary time. It's comparable to discretionary *income*—what you have left after you pay for housing, food, health care and such marginally satisfying expenses as taxes; discretionary *time* is what you have left after all the "have-to's."

If you're new in the business or the office, chances are a good deal of your time is taken up with command performances. It's part of paying your dues and earning future favors.

What remains is time you can spend as you like, time to spend working toward your goals, time to spend on activities of the highest priority—face-to-face contact with a decision-maker or preparing for that kind of commission-generating contact.

To avoid the danger of getting caught up in the nitty-gritty of office procedures, you need to create a fence around your discretionary time. That fence is your daily plan of action.

Phyllis Burhenn, a highly successful California agent says, "I always have my day scheduled. That's the last thing I do each evening.

When I plan the following day, I prepare a list, starting with the most important things that must be done. Then I evaluate my schedule to make sure it reflects my plans for the whole week. Too many people in this industry aren't willing to make the effort to prepare a plan to budget their time. I believe that without a game plan it's nearly impossible to accomplish anything in real estate." (Quoted in *Real Estate People*, by Robert Shook, Harper & Row.)

It is a well-documented fact that time you spend planning will pay you a 300 percent dividend. Every minute you spend planning a task or a project will save you three minutes in completing it. Twenty minutes of planning a job will save an hour of time in executing it.

If you spend 20 minutes to plan each day, you'll be investing 100 minutes a week and collecting a dividend of more than five hours of discretionary time every week. Over a year's time, that five-hour weekly bonus translates into 250 hours, the equivalent of five extra weeks if you plan on a 50-hour week. That's five extra weeks of income, five extra weeks to work toward achieving your goals, every year.

In ten years you will have saved the equivalent of an extra year. What was that annual income target you set a few chapters ago? $50,000? That's an extra $50,000 just for taking 20 minutes to plan what you're going to do each day. If you prefer a shorter horizon, think of it as a 10 percent bonus each year.

START WITH YOUR GOALS

Set a regular time for your daily planning session. A time when you can be alone, undisturbed and undistracted to think seriously about your goals and which ones you will address today—or tomorrow, if you reserve planning activities for the end of the day.

Some people get up early and plan their day at the breakfast table, before the family comes to the table; others get to the office early for their planning session. You may prefer to take 20 minutes at the end of the day, either at the office or at home. There are advantages to both. If you're a morning person, consider doing your planning early in the day, when you're fresh and ready to plan a vigorous day full of accomplishment. If you plan for tomorrow at the close of the day, chances are that events will still be fresh in your mind, and you can plan the actions that will bring negotiations to a successful close, for example. Or plan new approaches to bring buyers and sellers who are drifting apart back together again.

Whichever you choose, commit to that time every day. Make your planning session the first entry on each day's page in your planner, until it becomes such an ingrained part of your daily routine that you don't need a reminder.

Set Priorities

With your planner in front of you, look over your list of things to do. Concentrate on those you identified as As and insert them into your daily plan, allocating specific times for each one. If there aren't enough As to fill the available discretionary time, write in some Bs.

When you turn to the day's page, you will probably find you have already filled in some time slots with a sales meeting or preferably, a closing. You may have entered some appointments a week ago, as in Figure 6-1.

Earlier, we discussed the "mind dump," a term that makes up in precision what it lacks in elegance. It was an exercise to clear your mind of all the pressing demands crowding you, making it difficult to focus on any one task, much less to decide which one was most important and set a time to deal with the others.

You then sorted out the list and assigned A, B and C priorities to each item. That gave you the beginnings of an action plan. You knew what you had to do, and you identified the most important one. That's the list you should be working from as you enter items into your daily plan.

As you gain experience in managing your time, you will rely less and less on your to do list. You will have moved the items to your planner. And instead of listing new tasks as they occur or are assigned to you, you will write them down on a specific daily page in your planner under "to be done today."

That's a big step forward, because you'll be planning your time and your activities. Your tasks will be scheduled and spread out over time. Your to do list or mind dump should gradually—but steadily and as quickly as possible—find its way onto your daily pages of your planner.

Figure 6–1. Day-Timers™ page with some carryover activities and tickler file items.

		THURSDAY NOVEMBER, 1991		APPOINTMENTS & SCHEDULED EVENTS			
14			47 Days Left	HOURS	NAME	PLACE	SUBJECT
				7 / 0700			
				8 / 0800			
TO BE DONE TODAY (ACTION LIST)				9 / 0900			○
1 Make 10 phone calls				10 / 1000			
2 Get letters out to Katrow subdiv. res.				11 / 1100			
3 Outline presentation to Olde Towne const.				12 / 1200	Round Table Lunch with Tony G.		○
4 Talk to Jerry re finance course				1 / 1300	Meet Olsens at 1309 Waters		
5 Put up sign for Lynn at 1210 Waters				2 / 1400			
				3 / 1500			○
				4 / 1600			
				5 / 1700			○
				6 / 1800			
				7 / 1900			○
				8 / 2000			
				9 / 2100			
				10 / 2200			○
PHONE CALLS				EXPENSE & REIMBURSEMENT RECORD			

Illustration courtesy of Day-Timers™, Inc.

During your daily planning session, you should move those items over to "scheduled activities" so that you have allocated time to work on them. If you can't schedule a specific time, note it under "to be done today" until you figure out a time to do it.

Cut Big Jobs Down to Size

If you are assigned a big elephant of a task, you can't simply write "dispose of elephant" on a calendar page with any realistic hope of accomplishing it on that day. But you can find a day when there is a good chance you'll have an hour or two of time to yourself. If you can identify the time slot, great. On the lines for 10:00 A.M. to noon next Tuesday, for example, write "contemplate elephant." Then use that time to outline the task into its components or stages. Remember, the answer to the question "How do you eat an elephant?" is "One bite at a time."

Second best to scheduling a specific time to work on a project or attend to a task is to enter it under "things to be done today" at some future date in your planner. When the day comes and you start to actively contemplate the elephant and start thinking about cutting it into smaller pieces, insert them on future pages of your planner under "to be done today." Then when you plan that day's work, you can set a specific time to attend to it.

The difference between agreeing something needs to be done and setting a specific time to do it is the difference between "We really ought to meet for lunch," and "Let's meet for lunch at Clancy's tomorrow at noon." One is a vague intention—like a to do list. The other is a commitment to do a specific thing at a specific time and at a specific place.

An entry in your planner carries the force of commitment. We all have the power to delude ourselves, to say that we're going to clean out the basement—someday. Our intentions are honest enough. But intention without commitment, without a specific time, has no legs—it gets nowhere. But when you open your planner and see that you have committed to a task, you will keep your promise to yourself. The more specific the time for fulfilling the promise, the more powerful the commitment.

Plan To Address a Specific Goal

Turn back to your goals, which you wrote on special pages in your planner. Let's say one of those goals was to obtain at least two listings every month. It's the tenth of the month, and you haven't listed a property. In fact, you haven't really allocated time to pursuing listings. You know it's now time to get cracking.

You have a two-hour slot in the morning. How many phone calls can you make in two hours? Twenty? Thirty? Get out your prospect list and check the likeliest ones: those who replied to your cards offering an appraisal or who have indicated that they might be moving, or are interested in moving up.

Schedule the calls in your planner. Include your phone calls in the "to be done" column, along with other activities you plan for the day. But there may not be enough room.

A more effective way, which also provides a better record of results, is to block out the time for telephone calls under "appointments and scheduled events." That is now a commitment, *an appointment with yourself*, which you should treat as just as important as any other appointment. If someone tries to intrude on that time, say simply, "I'm sorry, I have an important commitment that hour."

List the people you're going to call during that hour, either on your "diary and work record" or on a "phone record" sheet. Although both are primarily designed to record completed tasks, they are well suited to listing tasks to be done and then checking them off as you accomplish them.

Note that in blocking out a time for phone calls, you are grouping similar activities, an important time-management technique. It increases your efficiency by eliminating the need to shift gears when you start dissimilar tasks. Calls to make listing appointments follow a similar pattern. You have your calling list in front of you, and you can go through without stopping to wonder whom to call next, prepare your questions and responses or decide whether you should be doing something else. You've made the time commitment, listed the people to call and know what you're going to say. Now all you have to do is follow through.

Use the same technique for other repetitive tasks. If you're going through the multilist to put together a tour, go through the process once and prepare as many tours as you have on your docket. It takes only a little more time to put three tours together than it does one. And you go through the list only once instead of three times.

MESHING WITH YOUR OFFICE'S SYSTEMS

On the assumption that you're not going to convert your entire office overnight to your way of doing things, you will probably need to integrate forms and methods used in your office with your system.

That ought not to present a large problem. For instance, many brokerages use a "listing follow-up" sheet to ensure that all the steps required for the timely sale of a listing are attended to. Another common form is one that lists and schedules the steps from signed agreement to closing. These are useful forms; however, they have a few weaknesses.

The first is that they can create a very fat planning book. They can also lead to an abundance of loose paper that keeps falling out of your planning book. Or they end up as a separate file that you have to thumb through frequently to make sure you're on top of everything.

By all means use the forms prescribed by your office. And use *your* system to schedule your day's work. For instance, an "agreement to closing schedule" might list the following events that you must plan for:

1. Deliver copies of the sales agreement to
   - Seller
   - Buyer
   - Attorneys
2. Notify Multilist of agreement
3. Obtain partial or total deposit and note any special conditions regarding interest
4. Make sure building inspections are performed:
   - Termite
   - Radon
   - Other
5. Provide documents to manager
   - Contract
   - Deposit
6. Install "sold" sign on property
7. Obtain mortgage application

8. Get comparable listings to bank appraiser
9. Obtain certificate of occupancy
10. Check on mortgage commitment
11. Give commission bill to _____
12. Confirm closing date

This is not intended as a complete list of all the events you will probably need to monitor after completing a sales agreement. Some geographical areas and some brokerages will require many more. Making sure that each one happens on time is critical; this ensures that you receive your commission on time and establishes you as an agent who rides herd on the details. They demonstrate the concern that will encourage both seller and buyer to provide referrals.

Listings usually require follow-up over a much longer period of time—unless you happen to be in a very hot real estate market and at this writing there aren't many of those. The listing follow-up sheet may fill both sides of a page and cover six months. These, too, are useful forms, but leafing through six months' worth of listings could take up your whole planning session and then some. It's therefore a good idea to transfer all those scheduled events into your planner. In that way, when you open to today's pages, you will find actions needed for each listing. You don't need to refer back to the listing follow-up sheet.

Consider All Your Goals

One of your goals was to secure two listings per month, and you scheduled activities that would move you toward that goal. But you still have some discretionary time that day, so let's look at another goal. You bought an audiocassette series on selling, which you were going to complete by the end of the month. It's going to take a half-hour to drive to your three o'clock appointment—just time enough to play one side of a cassette. Write "take sales cassette" on the 2:30 line. And just in case your appointment is delayed, take the next cassette, too; you can listen to it while you're waiting or driving back from the appointment.

Go through all your goals at each planning session and see which ones you can work on in open time slots that day. Always try to be prepared to use scraps of time. The ten-minute wait in the car is enough to write a few postcards. Or go through the multilist book to put together a tour for the client coming in next week. Or start making a phone list for tomorrow.

MAKE AN APPOINTMENT WITH YOURSELF

When you're caught up in the excitement and demands of the real estate business, it's easy to feel that you don't have time to think. Your daily planning session is one effective way to make sure you're addressing your goals, meeting your commitments and fulfilling your professional obligations.

How about time to review and update goals as we recommended earlier? When you start wondering whether you're on the right track and want to examine the path you're speeding down, you'll need more than the 20 minutes it takes to plan your day's work.

Go through your planner and find a block of time you devote to yourself. Write your name in the slot and treat that appointment with yourself as seriously as you would one with an important client.

Many working couples make such appointments with each other to make sure to discuss important questions involving them both. At first, it may sound overly formal to make an appointment with your spouse, but the frequent alternative is to defer important questions. And then postpone them again, and again, until they never get discussed. You continue to wonder whether you're doing the right things and you never get a satisfactory answer.

Your planner is one of the best ways to protect yourself against the tendency to procrastinate and the consequent stress and guilt.

WHEN THE WORLD WON'T RUN ACCORDING TO YOUR TIMETABLE

By now, your planner page probably looks something like the one in Figure 6-2.

You had your planning session at home, and you blocked out the first hour for correspondence and the next two hours for telephoning. You are meeting a mortgage lender for lunch to hear about some new creative financing structures. At 1:30, you're meeting new prospects, the Olsens, to show them some properties. You'll put up Lynn's sign on

Figure 6-2. Day-Timers™ page with sample "appointments and scheduled events."

14	THURSDAY NOVEMBER, 1991					APPOINTMENTS & SCHEDULED EVENTS		
					HOURS	NAME	PLACE	SUBJECT
					7 / 0700			
					8 / 0800			
TO BE DONE TODAY (ACTION LIST)					9 / 0900	② Letters to Katrow		
1	Make 10 phone calls				10 / 1000	① Get on the phone		
2	Get letters out to Katrow subdiv. res.				11 / 1100			
3	Outline presentation to Olde Towne Const.				12 / 1200	Round Table Lunch with Tony G.		
4	Talk to Jerry re finance course				1 / 1300	Meet Olsens at 1309 Waters for tour til 3:30?		
5	Put up sign for Lynn at 1210 Waters				2 / 1400			
					3 / 1500			
					4 / 1600	③ Outline O.T. presentation		
					5 / 1700			
					6 / 1800			
					7 / 1900			
					8 / 2000			
					9 / 2100			
					10 / 2200			
PHONE CALLS					**EXPENSE & REIMBURSEMENT RECORD**			

Illustration courtesy of Day-Timers™, Inc.

Plan Each Day's Activities 75

the way. The Olsens said they had to be back at work by 3:30 (for the closing of the New York Stock Exchange), but that one of them might be able to continue. That leaves two hours up in the air. Will you still be showing houses or will it be open time? You'll catch Jerry for a few minutes before lunch and, if the Olsens do leave at 3:30, you'll get back to the office and work on the Olde Towne presentation.

You've listed the calls you're going to make on a call record sheet. As you work your way through the phone calls and other items on your today list, check them off as completed. If you can't reach someone by the end of the day, roll it over to the next day during your next planning session.

If a phone call requires follow-up, schedule the day and time for follow-up immediately if possible. If you can't set a time, set a day and write in the action under "to be done today" on the next possible day. That's the tickler-reminder function of your planner.

If the call or activity produces some information, write it in your planner. Some people leave blank lines between tasks for this purpose. Another technique is to write the information on the first unused lines of the "diary and work record." Use the number of the item to relate the information you received to the activity that produced it. If "call Smith" was item 3, and you learned that the owner of 314 Liberty Street is being transferred, write 3 on the first open line and make a notation of what you learned. You can then plan to call the owner of 314 Liberty and write a thank-you note to Smith.

On this day, you get about halfway through your correspondence when the phone rings. It's your afternoon clients. You take the call. They've found some old college friends in a neighborhood that they'd previously crossed off as being too pricey for them. Could you arrange to...? This afternoon? You have two-and-a-half hours to put together a tour.

You push the correspondence aside with an arrow and tomorrow's date—you'll finish it then. You check the multilist to see what's available in the new neighborhood for your clients and get on the phone. You're able to make three appointments and find six more that look possible. You decide you'll show the three and give them a tour of neighborhood, pointing out the other six. And you make a mental note to probe. Can they afford this neighborhood? What are they really looking for? You need time.

It's now 10:45. The boss walks in and wants you to participate in a preliminary visit to a new executive estate development. At 4:00!

Time To Look at Options and Priorities

The day isn't going according to plan. You got only halfway through your correspondence and used up an hour of your phone time, thinking you had a good chance to get back to it in the late afternoon. Now that's thrown into question.

How important is that lunch? Can someone go in your place? How about that 4:00 presentation? It sounds important, but what is your role in it? Can it be postponed? Can you arrive late? Will you be responsible for preparing the dog-and-pony show? Can the boss say you'll call tomorrow? Is tomorrow going to be better? You can clean up your correspondence tonight, but can you get back on your phone schedule tomorrow?

These types of dilemmas come up regularly in real estate. The only effective way to deal with them is to have a clear understanding of your own priorities so you can make decisions consistent with your goals.

The face-to-face appointment with prospects—even though it shredded your plans—takes precedence over all the disturbances. Everything else is negotiable. What is illustrated here is that though the plan itself may be modified or even destroyed, this in no way diminishes the importance of planning. Without the plan, which reflects your goals, you would not have the data needed to make an informed decision.

Make sure your "diary and work record" reflects the changes and includes notations that will help you plan to attend to new items during your next planning session.

Make "Command Performances" Serve Your Goals

Another day might show a caravan is scheduled and you're expected to attend. If you had your druthers, you would rather show houses that just came on the market to a hard-to-impress prospect.

Though the main purpose of a caravan is to familiarize you with what's on the market, you can make caravan time work harder for you. Bring your planner with you and relate what you see to what that buyer has been saying he or she wants. When you do get to that buyer, you'll have an additional house or two to show. Write down the salient features of the homes you see to make your call that much more effective and persuasive.

The same is true of sales meetings. If your meetings are round tables, you can pick up golden nuggets of wisdom or information that you can apply to specific situations in your selling. The prospective buyers with a house they've been trying to sell for six months could be swayed by a new wrinkle in bridge financing. If the meeting really drifts off into never-never land—as all too many do—have your planner with you. No one needs to know you're "considering the elephant" that we encountered earlier. They may think you're madly taking notes on the less-than-fascinating presentation. But you can use the time that would otherwise be wasted to work on an important project.

Some real estate agents get more than others from sitting open houses. For some, it's no more than a necessary—and onerous—chore. Others pick up leads on houses coming up, on prospects whose requirements are changing, on reactions to various amenities. Even neighbors who are "just curious" can provide useful insights.

So put on your game face and come ready to play. Good time management includes seizing the moment and following leads that come up unexpectedly. Stick to your schedule but stay alert to surprise opportunities. Focus on your goals, but don't put blinders on.

THE GENTLE ART OF SAYING NO

No is probably the most important word in time management. Few people use it enough or at the right time.

In the genial and friendly atmosphere of a real estate office, it's very easy to take on other people's work and responsibilities. "Will you sit my open house?" "Can you swing by and put up the sign at 2137 Oak Lane?" "I have a hair appointment; could you take my floor time this afternoon?"

Most everyone enjoys helping others; it's one of the reasons you went into real estate in the first place. But another equally important reason is that it's a business where you are rewarded almost in direct proportion to your own efforts. The number of properties you list reflects the time and effort you put into obtaining them.

Does that mean that you should only look out for your own gain and rewards? Not at all. It means that you must keep your goals and priorities in front of you at all times. (Remember that not all goals and priorities need relate directly to career and professional advancement.)

Then when someone asks you to do something, you can ask yourself which one of your goals and objectives would be served by taking on the task. If you can see no relationship between the request and your goals, you have a rational basis for declining.

You don't have to say, "Sorry, but what you're asking me to do in no way serves my self-interest." But you can say, after looking in your planner, "I have to be at the other end of town that afternoon for a meeting I set up weeks ago. Perhaps some other time."

You've offered a good reason why you can't oblige and left the door open for a future favor. Most people in the real estate business have to rely on others to cover bases for them occasionally. Yet it's important to have a standard by which to determine when to oblige and when to say no. Your written goals and objectives form the basis of that criterion. They enable you to say no without offense when no is the correct response.

Your time log will also tell you who asks for more favors than seems ready to return. And when you need a favor, you'll have a pretty good idea of whom you have a right to ask.

Protect Your Goals and They Will Protect You

Most people have trouble saying no the boss, even the most inconsistent and unreasonable one. Of course. Most of us are "people pleasers" at heart and we know the importance of pleasing the boss.

But sometimes we must say no to the boss and risk incurring his or her displeasure. Here again, your goals will minimize the risk and even raise you up in the boss's esteem.

The principal reason for setting goals with the boss's help and concurrence is to benefit from his or her knowledge, as well as to set goals that are agreeable to both you and the boss. They are your goals, but they support the organization's goals.

Then if the boss wants you to do something that interferes with your plans and thereby jeopardizes achieving your goals, you have an effective reply. When the boss upsets *your* game plan, the game plan of the organization is upset. And that causes wheel spinning, which is a waste of time. It also creates unnecessary tension in the office, which may be the biggest time-waster of all.

So, when the boss asks you to cover the phones, prepare some ads for someone else's listings, or do anything that's miles from what you had planned for the day, you have recourse to his or her self-interest. You look at your planner, look at your sales goals and say something like, "Gee, that sounds like a neat assignment, but if I'm going to meet the goals we agreed on for July, I should really spend two hours on the phone (or at my farm) that day, and the rest of the day is booked solid. Is there another time I could help you?"

You've reminded the boss that you're focusing on objectives jointly arrived at, while demonstrating your desire to help. It may not work every time, but the most irrational boss will eventually recognize the importance of associates' goals. The best defense against a boss who tries, unwittingly or wittingly, to pull you away from your goals and the plans that support them, is to remind him that they are *his or her* goals as well.

The Boss Has To Say No, Too

The gentle art of saying no is indispensable if you want to use your time wisely, which is to say to achieve your goals. If you are the boss, the trap you have to avoid is upward delegation: letting subordinates put "the monkey on your back," as William Oncken puts it.

If you offer to hear a subordinate's problem out and say you'll think about it, you have just taken on the problem. Your subordinate has stopped thinking about it. What was his or her problem is now yours.

A more appropriate response is to acknowledge the problem, suggest directions and resources that can help solve it and set a time for the person to return with several possible solutions. That approach to subordinates' problems sends the responsibility for finding solutions back with the person who has the problem and preserves your role as one with the experience and wisdom to select the most desirable approach.

As boss, manager or broker, you cannot afford to spend your time solving other people's problems. You have a responsibility to *help* solve problems or choose one of several proposed solutions. That's very different from solving them. One is a front-line role, the other is a staff role. As a manager, you probably have to serve in both roles—but at different times!

You probably have the experience to solve problems more quickly than your associates. And it can be very frustrating to watch someone struggle for days with a problem you could resolve in an hour with a few well-placed phone calls. But learn to stand back. If you make a habit of solving your associates' problems, you may soon find yourself doing little else. And your associates will not develop the problem-solving ability.

Delegation and keeping responsibility where it belongs is discussed at greater length in Chapter 10.

CHAPTER 7

Match Your Performance to Your Goals

In Chapter 4, you listed your various job responsibilities and started to think about how much time you felt you ought to devote to each one. Now it's time to take a look at where the time actually goes, because in this chapter, you will see how to bring your actual performance in line with your projections.

These two steps could be the most important in your self-management program, because they will reveal and *quantify* precisely the time-wasting, nonproductive activities that are derailing you from your plan. You'll be able to identify and measure all those little diversions that lead nowhere. More important, this analysis will give you the means to attack the problem at its source, whatever, wherever or *who*ever it is.

THE 80–20 TRAP

In the last century, an Italian economist and sociologist named Pareto maintained that the wealthiest 20 percent of the population accounted for 80 percent of the wealth. This meant that the other 80 percent of the people shared only the remaining 20 percent of the wealth. It also meant that the average individual among the "significant few," as Pareto called them, had *16* times as much as the average member of the less wealthy.

Although his ideas have been debated ever since, Pareto's Law, as it is sometimes called, seems to apply to many economic phenomena. For instance, 20 percent of a manufacturer's product line generates 80 percent of the profit. Twenty percent of any alumni group gives 80 percent of the funds. Recent data on the distribution of wealth in the United States is even more skewed toward the upper brackets than Pareto posited: The IRS reported in 1990 that the wealthiest 1.6 percent of the population held 28.5 percent of the wealth.

And in many businesses, 20 percent of the sales force generates 80 percent of the sales. That may or may not be true in your office, but the A, B and C values we assigned to various real estate tasks suggest a reason for this imbalance. Most agents spend by far the largest share of their time on Bs and Cs. A relatively small percentage of the average agent's time is devoted to A activities—the *only* activities that generate income. We saw early that some agents feel 5 percent is pretty good. Isn't it likely that high earners manage more face-to-face time with correspondingly better results? Let's look into it.

START WITH A TIME LOG

The place to look is in a record of how you now spend your time. Before you can correct anything, you need to look at the present situation. You need to record in great detail how you spend your time.

One of the requisite functions of your personal management system, discussed in Chapter 5, was that it incorporate a time log. A time log is nothing more than a record of what you did during each segment of the day. Use any time segment with which you feel comfortable, but the most workable is tenths of an hour—six-minute segments. It's easier to convert percentages into tenths of an hour and vice-versa than five-minute segments (twelfths of an hour), which are awkward, or quarter-hours, which are too large a unit.

The "diary and work record" section of the two-page-per-day Day-Timers™ Junior Desk Planner is based on tenths of an hour. If you use that section to list phone calls to be made, all you need to do is write in the time you spend as you make each call (Figure 7–1). You should keep your time log in "real time," i.e., jot down the activity *as you do it*, not at the end of the day. Your time log must be factual to be useful; if you trust your memory, you'll write down what you *think* you did, or

Match Your Performance to Your Goals

Figure 7-1. Diary and work record as time log.

REF.	NAME OR PROJECT	DETAILS OF MEETINGS - AGREEMENTS - DECISIONS	TIME HRS. 1/10
		DIARY AND WORK RECORD — 46th Week / 318th Day — **THURSDAY** NOVEMBER, 1991 — **14**	
1		B letter to Walters	.2
2		B letter to Camerons	.2
3		B letter to Stewarts	.2
4		B call from Olsens	.2
5		B review multilist	.6
6		B calling for app'ts to show	.3
7		C talking with Stacy re presenta-	
8		tion this P.M.!	.3
9		B calling for app'ts to show	.7
10		waiting for call backs	
11		B letter to Meads	.3
12		B letter to Sharps	.3
13		B letter to Owens	.3
14		NO LUNCH!	
15		C Driving to Olsen app't	.3
16		C Put up sign for Lynn	.1
17		A Showing Olsens around	1.6
18		can put $40,000 down	
19		and meet $1,300 payment!	
20		C Drive back to office	.3
21		C Outlining presentation	1.7
22		C Saw Jerry about finance	.1
23		C Talking with Stacy about	
24		his presentation	.8
25		make app't to discuss	
26		next week	

Illustration courtesy of Day-Timers™, Inc.

what you *ought* to have done. You need to know what you *did* and when.

Few people really know how they spend their time until they keep a time log. Ask them, and they'll give you an idealized picture of constant productive motion. They forget all the interruptions and diversions. They delude themselves that they are always focused on the most important and rewarding tasks. Delusions are a poor launching pad from which to reach your goals.

The important thing is to know how you're spending your time, why you spend your time on certain things, and what those activities produce. Then you're in a position to evaluate your activities and make the changes that will achieve your goals.

You also need to categorize your various activities so that you label each line appropriately. Here's a suggested breakdown by category, using the A, B and C time classifications.

_____ Telephoning for appointments with potential listers

_____ Making personal calls in your farm area

_____ Compiling listings for prospective buyers

_____ Talking with potential listers

_____ Caravaning

_____ Sitting open houses

_____ Showing houses to prospective buyers

_____ Scanning the multilist book or computer

_____ Phone duty at the office

_____ Typing up offers

_____ Attending closings

_____ Presenting/negotiating offers

_____ Attending meetings

_____ Training new associates

_____ Mailing cards and other reminders to prospects

_____ Preparing advertisements to promote listings

_____ Obtaining appraisals

_____ Previewing homes

_____ Messengering

_____ Arranging for inspections

_____ Calling attorneys

_____ Calling banks and other lenders

_____ Calling on buyers' new neighbors

_____ Qualifying buyers

_____ Attending planning boards for leads on new tracts

_____ Taking real estate courses

_____ Obtaining certificates of occupancy

_____ _____

_____ _____

_____ _____

It's easy to see why so many people spend so much time on non-income-producing activities. There are so many of them!

As you make your time-log entries, assign A, B, C or D to each one. You may have your own ideas about classifying them, and you'll probably perform many tasks not mentioned here. But you know the criteria, so you can assign each activity to the proper category. Don't forget to include D time spent during the day.

Later in this chapter, when you analyze your time use, you'll need a more precise classification of activities. So in addition to A, B, C and D classifications, assign a number to each activity: *1* for showing, *2* for listing, *3* for cold-calling and so on. The importance of this slight complication will become evident when you analyze and try to improve performance.

Keep your time log for four weeks. Then take the average amount of time per week you spent on each category. That is your present time-use performance picture. Be sure to include interruptions, coffee breaks and other time-wasters so that you have a factual record of how you spend your time.

Does your time log show that you spend practically all of your time on low-reward activities? And you thought you were really plugged into the right activities! If you weren't producing the sales and listings to reach your income goal, you now have a clue as to why.

SMALL ADJUSTMENT, BIG RESULTS

Unless you're wildly short of your income goals, chances are that a fairly modest adjustment in your daily work pattern will bring about startling increases in your productivity.

Easier said than done? Probably. Worth the effort? Absolutely! Here's why: Let's say that your time log shows you spend 10 percent of your time face-to-face with prospective listers or buyers, and another 20 percent at tasks that prepare you to meet prospects—making phone calls, sending postcards, putting together lists of properties to show, etc. The other 70 percent is taken up by activities that, though necessary, do not produce income.

And let's say you're averaging $25,000 a year with that kind of time distribution. If you're working 50 hours a week and A time accounts for 10 percent, you're spending five hours a week face-to-face with clients.

Now suppose you increase that face-to-face time by just *one hour per week*. That's an increase of 20 percent in your A time. And that should increase your earnings proportionately—by 20 percent. Therefore, that additional hour of face time each week has the potential to increase your annual income by $5,000.

Adding that one hour without prolonging your working week may call for some negotiation—with your boss, your family or yourself. It has to come from somewhere. You're the best judge of where it can come from, and your time log will give you important clues.

If you've been conscientious about tracking your time throughout the day, every day for four weeks, you can identify the time-wasters. Maybe you're allowing yourself to be trapped into "playing office." Or doing someone else's work. Or letting conversations drag on.

It may not be practical to add the increment of face time without fine-tuning your overall pattern of work. And that probably can't be done overnight.

You can, however, probably up the hours you spend on activities that lead to face time, which in the long run will produce the same results.

Your goal should be to maximize the time you spend face-to-face with prospects.

ANALYZING AND ADJUSTING YOUR TIME-USE PERFORMANCE

You now have a record of how you spent your time over four weeks, and you have calculated the average amount of time you spent on various aspects of your job during that typical period.

How does it look? How does it compare with the tentative commitments you made in Chapter 4? How much time did you spend face-to-face with prospective buyers and listers? How much time working your farm? Floor time? Servicing your listings?

Are you satisfied with the distribution, or is it heavy with C time and activities that don't produce income? Let's see if we can make adjustments and shift some of that C time up to B, and some of that B time up to A.

Set Up Detailed Categories

You can analyze your time in terms of A, B and C time and tasks; a more precise picture of your present performance, however, will help you pinpoint areas where you can improve. So instead of A, B and C, let's number the major categories. Even though we're looking to make macro shifts up the scale, you're really trying to reduce the time you spend on specific nonproductive tasks. Therefore, we'll pull some tasks from our earlier list of real estate–related duties and number them.

1. Showing houses to a prospective buyer
2. Talking to an owner who is ready to sell
3. Lining up listings
4. Making appointments to show or discuss listing

5. Preparing listing papers
6. Servicing listings (covers a variety of tasks)
7. Cold-calling in your farm residents
8. Correspondence
9. Attending sales meetings
10. Updating records
11. Calling mortgage lenders
12. Working caravans
13. Sitting open houses
14. Working floor time
15. Making introductory appraisals
16. All activities not related to real estate

If this list doesn't fit your exact requirements, delete, add or adjust to reflect the activities you recorded in your time log. Be sure to track activities not related to real estate and include them in your analysis. You need to know how much work time you're losing.

Write these categories down so you can track your performance for the next four weeks. The time analysis form illustrated in Figure 7-2 was designed for this purpose and provides the lines and columns to conduct your analysis over the four-week period, during which you will continue to keep your time log. The difference is that instead of merely recording, you'll be making a conscious effort to make those upward shifts. The form will make it easy to see how you're doing.

In keeping your time log for the next four weeks, include numbers for each task to match those on the list you prepared. That will facilitate calculating hours devoted to each task.

Calculate the Percentage of Time on Each Category

Once you have written the categories in your time analysis sheet or form, enter the average number of hours you devoted to each task during your initial four-week time log. Also calculate and record the percentage of your total work time those hours represent.

If you're using the form illustrated here, you will have filled in the first four columns: the task number, task name, hours spent on that task and the percentage. For instance, if you averaged 55 hours per week and spent an average 5.5 hours working your farm, that's 10 per-

Match Your Performance to Your Goals

Figure 7-2. Day-Timers™ time analysis form with 16 categories written in.

NAME: Angela Putnam
FROM Aug. 4 TO Aug. 31
PLANNED WORK HOURS: 50

AREAS OF RESPONSIBILITY OR CATEGORIES:
1. Showing Properties
2. Talking to Prospective Listers
3. Lining up Listings
4. Making appts to list or show
5. Preparing listing papers
6. Serving listings
7. Cold-Calling on farm
8. Correspondence
9. Sales Meetings
10. Updating records
11. Calling mortgage lenders
12. Caravans
13. Open Houses
14. Floor time
15. Introductory appraisals
16. Non-real estate activities

TIME ANALYSIS

Illustration courtesy of Day-Timers™, Inc.

cent. On line 7 you would enter 5.5 hours in the third (present time) column and 10 in the next (%) column, since 5.5 is 10 percent of 55.

Do the same for every category you listed. Write in the hours devoted to each task and the percentage so that you have a record of your present performance that resembles Figure 7-3.

Push for Your Ideal

Note that the upper right-hand corner of the form has a space for planned work hours. Be sure to record that number on the form you use to remind you of the hours you intend to devote to your real estate work.

The next two columns on the time analysis form are for the ideal number of hours and percentage of total time for each task. The person whose form we're using had planned to work 50 hours a week but actually worked 55 as shown in the bottom line. She had no "open time," as shown in the line above. Some adjustments are called for.

With your four-week performance record in front of you, look at the calculations you made in Chapter 3, where you translated your income target into tasks. That will help you determine the time required to accomplish those tasks. Now estimate the *percentage* of your total work week you should devote to each task to generate your targeted income goal.

Write in a percentage for each numbered task on the appropriate line in the sixth column. Then multiply your total time commitment by that percentage to get the ideal number of hours to be devoted to each task. It's easier to estimate the percentage first and then calculate the hours than the other way around. Remember that your percentages should total 100, and your total hours should equal your planned work hours. Your time analysis sheet should now look something like that in Figure 7-4.

CONFORM THE REAL WORLD TO YOUR IDEAL

You have now created an ideal structure that includes the time you intend to work so that you have time to pursue your other goals. And you have allocated time to the various parts of your job so that you achieve your professional and income goals.

Figure 7-3. Day-Timers™ time analysis form with the average number of hours spent on each category over a four-week period and the percentage of total hours for each category calculated.

NAME: Angela Putnam
FROM: Aug. 4 TO: Aug. 31
PLANNED WORK HOURS: 50

NO	AREAS OF RESPONSIBILITY OR CATEGORIES	PRESENT TIME	%	IDEAL TIME	WEEK 1 ACTUAL TIME	WEEK 2 ACTUAL TIME	WEEK 3 ACTUAL TIME	WEEK 4 ACTUAL TIME	TOTAL ACTUAL TIME	%	NEW IDEAL TIME	%
1	Showing Properties	3.9	7									
2	Talking to Prospective Listers	6.7	12									
3	Lining up Listings	2.8	5									
4	Making appts to list or show	3.7	7									
5	Preparing listing papers	2.6	5									
6	Serving listings	3.4	6									
7	Cold-Calling on Farm	5.5	10									
8	Correspondence	1.8	3									
9	Sales Meetings	2.0	4									
10	Updating records	1.7	3									
11	Calling Mortgage lenders	1.9	3									
12	Caravans	3.7	7									
13	Open Houses	4.0	7									
14	Floor time	4.0	7									
15	Introductory Appraisals	3.7	7									
16	Non-real estate activities	3.6	7									

REMARKS
OPEN TIME
TOTAL TIME: 55.0 / 100

TIME ANALYSIS

Illustration courtesy of Day-Timers™, Inc.

Figure 7-4. Day-Timers™ time analysis form with ideal time use and percentages calculated.

NAME: Angela Putnam FROM: Aug. 4 TO: Aug. 31 PLANNED WORK HOURS: 50

TIME ANALYSIS

NO	AREAS OF RESPONSIBILITY OR CATEGORIES	PRESENT TIME	%	IDEAL TIME	%	WEEK 1 ACTUAL TIME	WEEK 2 ACTUAL TIME	WEEK 3 ACTUAL TIME	WEEK 4 ACTUAL TIME	TOTAL ACTUAL TIME	%	NEW IDEAL TIME	%
1	Showing Properties	3.9	7	5.0	10								
2	Talking to Prospective Listers	6.7	12	7.5	15								
3	Lining up Listings	2.8	5	2.5	5								
4	Making appts. to list or show	3.7	7	5.0	10								
5	Preparing listing papers	2.6	5	3.0	6								
6	Serving listings	3.4	6	2.5	5								
7	Cold-Calling on farm	5.5	10	5.0	10								
8	Correspondence	1.8	3	2.0	4								
9	Sales Meetings	2.0	4	2.0	4								
10	Updating records	1.7	3	1.0	2								
11	Calling mortgage lenders	1.9	3	1.0	2								
12	Caravans	3.7	7	2.5	5								
13	Open Houses	4.0	7	4.0	8								
14	Floor-time	4.0	7	4.0	8								
15	Introductory appraisals	3.7	7	2.0	4								
16	Non-real estate activities	3.6	7	1.0	2								

REMARKS — OPEN TIME
TOTAL TIME: 55 / 100 / 50.0 / 100

Illustration courtesy of Day-Timers™, Inc.

The next step is to put it to work. Continue to keep your time log for the next four weeks. At the end of each week, tote up the hours you spent at various tasks and insert those totals in the four "actual time" slots for weeks 1, 2, 3 and 4.

As you insert the weekly numbers, compare them with your ideal. They probably won't match the first week, so try to do better the second week. And the third and the fourth. You should be coming closer.

At the end of your fourth week, calculate your new average in each category and insert those numbers in the "actual time" column under "total" and calculate the percentages and insert them in the adjacent "%" column.

You can now compare your time-use performance for the four weeks *before* you determined your ideal with your performance in the four-week period during which you were trying to meet your ideal. Your sheet should resemble Figure 7-5, with all the columns filled in except the last two.

Because no two weeks are alike in real estate, the four-week average is a more significant measure of your progress than any of the individual weeks. How close is your four-week average to your ideal? Is it closer to the ideal than your "present time" figure, the one you calculated before you began to analyze your time use? How difficult was it to stick to your time-use projections?

On the basis of your four-week record, a period during which you were making a conscious effort to focus on predetermined activities for a specified number of hours each week, you are now in a position to re-evaluate your commitments and calculate a new ideal, if necessary. Then insert those numbers in the last two columns on your time analysis sheet.

Once you calculate the new ideals, begin another four-week cycle during which you will try to conform to your revised time commitments. Use your "new ideal time."

Remember that your time analysis is based on the calculations you made in Chapter 3. Therefore, if you find that you were unable to make the calls to produce the number of listings you calculated, you may have to allocate more time to that activity. If you aren't meeting your ideal number of hours in face-to-face meetings with buyers, you may have to juggle some other activities in order to either attract more prospective buyers or spend more time with the prospects you have.

Figure 7-5. Day-Timers™ time analysis form with actual and total time use and percentages calculated over a four-week period.

NAME: Angela Putnam
FROM: Aug. 4 TO Aug. 31
PLANNED WORK HOURS: 50

NO.	AREAS OF RESPONSIBILITY OR CATEGORIES	PRESENT TIME	%	IDEAL TIME	%	WEEK 1 ACTUAL TIME	WEEK 2 ACTUAL TIME	WEEK 3 ACTUAL TIME	WEEK 4 ACTUAL TIME	TOTAL ACTUAL TIME	%	NEW IDEAL TIME	%
1	Showing properties	3.9	7	5.0	10	3.1	5.5	2.8	7.3	4.7	9		
2	Talking to Prospective Listers	6.7	12	7.5	15	6.2	7.4	8.0	4.5	6.5	12		
3	Lining up Listings	2.8	5	2.5	5	4.7	2.4	2.6	2.2	3.0	6		
4	Making appts. to list or show	3.7	7	5.0	10	3.2	3.8	6.7	4.8	4.6	9		
5	Preparing listing papers	2.6	5	3.0	6	1.9	2.8	3.8	3.1	2.9	5		
6	Serving listings	3.4	6	2.5	5	3.5	3.2	2.8	2.6	3.2	6		
7	Cold-calling on farm	5.5	10	5.0	10	6.2	5.7	5.4	4.7	5.5	10		
8	Correspondence	1.8	3	2.0	4	2.2	2.6	1.4	2.9	2.3	4		
9	Sales meetings	2.0	4	2.0	4	2.0	2.0	2.0	2.6	2.0	4		
10	Updating Records	1.7	3	1.0	2	1.2	1.5	1.2	1.0	1.2	2		
11	Calling Mortgage Lenders	1.9	3	1.0	2	1.4	.5	1.3	1.6	1.2	2		
12	Caravans	3.7	7	2.5	5	2.9	2.9	3.1	3.3	3.1	6		
13	Open Houses	4.0	7	4.0	8	6.0	4.0	4.0	4.0	4.5	8		
14	Floor-time	4.0	7	4.0	8	6.0	4.0	4.0	8.0	5.5	10		
15	Introductory appraisals	3.7	7	2.0	4	3.2	3.6	2.4	1.4	2.7	5		
16	Non-real estate activities	3.6	7	1.0	2	1.5	1.6	1.0	.7	1.2	2		
	TOTAL TIME	55.0	100	50.0	100	55.2	53.5	52.5	54.3	53.9			

TIME ANALYSIS — REMARKS / OPEN TIME

DAY-TIMERS, Inc. ALLENTOWN, PA 18195 · STYLE L482 · PRODUCT NO. 92137 · COPYRIGHT 1988 - 1988 PRINTED IN USA

Illustration courtesy of Day-Timers™, Inc.

Neither radical surgery nor overnight reform are practical. You have to deal with your own ingrained habits as well as the company culture.

YOU ARE NOW IN CONTROL

The process of time analysis is designed to put you in control of how you spend your time so that you can achieve your goals. In the previous examples, we have focused on real estate activities with a view to maximizing the time you spend on those activities that produce income.

If your projections were valid, you should see yourself steadily approaching your income goal. If, on the other hand, you do not see that kind of progress, you may have to reconsider your commitments and even your priorities.

If you can't reduce the hours you spend on C activities and switch them to A or B, you may have to increase the hours you devote to your real estate work. Or you may decide to modify your income projections. But that is now a conscious decision on your part. You make the choice based on your priorities and goals.

Before you bite that bullet, though, take a good look at your time analysis sheet and see how much D time is creeping into working hours. If it's more than an hour a week, the problem may not be with your projections and priorities but with distractions. It's possible you're not actually working the number of hours you committed to, which may or may not be your fault. The next chapter offers suggestions for dealing with things that interfere with meeting your commitments.

CHAPTER 8

The Urge To Procrastinate: How To Curb It; How To Use It

Don Marquis, creator of Archie, the cockroach who wooed a mouse named Mehitabel with letters he typed by diving onto the keys, a laborious process that precluded capital letters, defined procrastination as "the art of keeping up with yesterday." Perhaps more to the point is Edward Young's declaration that "procrastination is the thief of time."

After "interruptions," the most common complaint heard from people who have trouble doing what they're supposed to do when they're supposed to do it is procrastination.

Most of us have trouble keeping up with today; yesterday is too late. And too frequently, we feel robbed at the end of the day, because we see that we have more things to do than we had when we started. A conscientious time log will enlighten us as to where the time went. But that isn't exactly the same thing as understanding why we didn't do what we had intended or hoped to do.

In its simplest and most virulent form, procrastination begins with, "I'll do it later." And later and later and later. In other words, the longer we put off a task, the harder doing it becomes. Everybody has told us that.

The easy solution is to do it now. But is it really that easy? In fact, "doing it now" may in itself be a form of procrastination if it diverts us from a more important task.

WHY DO WE PROCRASTINATE?

We give ourselves many reasons for procrastinating. I'm busy. I forgot. It's boring. There wasn't time. I had a visitor. The boss asked me to _____ (fill in whatever is appropriate).

"Too busy" is a good reason, provided you were busy with a task you had consciously determined was more important than what you deferred.

"Forgetting" is usually unacceptable and frequently unpardonable. Someone was probably depending on you, and you have failed him or her. Shame on you. Next time, if there is a next time, write the task in your planner.

"Boring" can be overcome by focusing on the rewards to come from the task.

"There wasn't time" reflects a need for better planning. Either you didn't allow enough time for the task or you let another task encroach on the time you set aside.

"I had a visitor" *may* be a good reason if the visitor represented A time and you had scheduled a B or C activity.

A special assignment from the boss comes under the heading of *force majeure*, something you can't anticipate or do much about. We did discuss appealing to the boss's self-interest in Chapter 6; that, too, is based on planning, which as you may have begun to suspect, is what we've been leading up to from the beginning.

Another major cause of procrastination is fear of failure. A task that lies outside our experience can make us feel overwhelmed.

For instance, recently promoted managers often suffer acute discomfort when confronted with their new responsibilities. They were promoted because they were successful agents. They knew how to persuade prospective sellers that their listings would sell promptly at the right price. They were skilled in fathoming buyers' unstated needs and limitations and uncovering properties that joined all the dots and created the exact picture the buyers had in mind.

But that superlative sales performance has nothing to do with budgeting, hiring and firing, training, motivating, adjudicating squabbles and all the other managerial functions of which most of us aren't aware until we are managers.

When suddenly confronted with these unfamiliar tasks, we tend to retreat to familiar territory and become involved in tasks where we can shine. And managing? We procrastinate. We become so absorbed in doing what we do well that we plan to take care of it later, run out of time or any of the other reasons given earlier for not attending to our new and somewhat intimidating responsibilities.

The pattern is repeated in all industries and at all levels. The president promoted out of sales insists on playing sales manager instead of planning the company's future. The marketing vice president who came out of data processing spends her time reading printouts instead of identifying new markets and new needs in old markets.

WHAT DOES THE TASK CONSIST OF?

Every big task and every big problem consists of a number of smaller tasks or smaller problems. Just as there are steps in selling a house, there are component skills and responsibilities in managing an office or building a skyscraper or selling leases in a shopping mall.

The new task in front of you is there because someone thought you had the *background* to learn the new skills required to do the task. If budgeting, for instance, is part of the job, it's a skill you can learn. The local community college probably offers courses. Or you could get help from a manager in another area.

Once you have broken the assignment down into its components, you can allocate time to address each one separately. Such a process accomplishes two things: it reduces the big problem to a series of smaller manageable problems; and it sets aside time for dealing with each part of the problem.

You have now broken your elephant-sized task down into manageable bite-sized subtasks. You have set aside time to deal with each one. Will those really cure procrastination? They will help, because they provide a way to deal with the task you wanted to avoid.

There's one more important step that should ensure accomplishing those subtasks on the way to completing the larger, formerly intimidating task.

Parkinson's Law states that work will expand to fill the time available. If you tell your teenage son to clean out the garage without specifying *when* you want it cleaned, chances are it won't be done until you make clear your time expectations. He won't assign a high priority to the task.

If you say, "Clean the garage out Saturday," you'd better check about two hours before sundown to verify progress, because your son will probably do what we all do with low-priority items: procrastinate.

Let's try a slightly different approach. Friday night, tell your son that you are taking the car out for two hours at ten o'clock Saturday; when you come back, you expect to see the garage cleaned. If you also offer a reward for timely completion, chances are good that you will find a clean garage on your return.

The final step in ensuring completion of any task is to set a deadline. Set a realistic deadline and stick to it. Block the time out in your planner and let nothing interfere with finishing the work at the time you set.

Of course, it won't always work out that way. The task may take longer than you planned. If so, reschedule the completion date and block out the time to work on it. If you finish ahead of schedule, try to attack the next part of the problem. Or use the time gained to work on another project. Don't let the Parkinson's Law take over so that you lose the benefit of early completion.

The same guidelines apply when trying to solve an unfamiliar problem or to acquire a new skill. Create a timetable for yourself that shows on what day and at what time you will attack each portion of the problem. And set a time for completing each task.

BECOME AN EXPERT TIME ESTIMATOR

The biggest rewards go to those who learn to make accurate estimates of how long it takes to do things. Accurate time estimates enable you to schedule your work with minimum time loss. If you overestimate time requirements by 25 percent, you risk losing 25 percent of your available time. If you underestimate, you'll be trying to catch up with yourself all the time, a highly stressful way to live.

Your time log will show you how long it took you to do similar tasks in the past. Use it as a guide to estimating future time requirements. The exercise will be invaluable in analyzing time use and matching your performance to your goals. You will be able to allocate time to the various aspects of your work and arrive at your ideal allocations that much more easily.

Set Shorter and Shorter Deadlines

If a task took two hours last week, plan to do it in an hour-and-a-half next time. And then an hour. The benefit is more than just the time saved.

First, it will accomplish the interrelated twin goals of time management—working smarter instead of harder and accomplishing more in less time.

Second, and perhaps more important, it will help you work more accurately. If that sounds strange, consider this: Working to a tight schedule means there isn't time to do it over; you have to get it right the first time. While that hard-to-swallow theory comes from industry, it has application in other endeavors. Underlying the theory is—would you believe—*planning!*

Back in Chapter 6, we said that one minute spent planning a job saves three minutes doing the job. And dividends keep coming. As your planning becomes ever more precise, based on increased knowledge, experience and confidence, you can accomplish more and more in less and less time. What took you all day the first time you tried, you can now do in a morning. Or two hours.

It may be true that everything is always more difficult, takes longer and costs more than we expected. But if you learn to make accurate time estimates and treat deadlines as sacred commitments, you will prosper while others flounder and languish.

Each successfully completed assignment adds to your skill. So why not raise your expectations of yourself? Keep shortening the deadline. You may amaze yourself.

PROCRASTINATION IS NOT ALWAYS A DIRTY WORD

We organize tasks into categories A, B and C, with A being the most important because they are the only ones that can generate commissions. They are the ones to focus your time and energy on.

What about the others? They can wait. They must wait. They will wait.

You need to go through all your As and decide which *one* of them is the most important. If you have more than three or four As, you need either to apply tougher criteria based on potential reward or you need to delegate. The task you decide is *most* important in terms of reward is your A-1.

Concentrate on your A-1. Work on it until it is done; don't let anything divert you. Stick by your decision. Everything else must *wait* until you accomplish that "most important task."

If you succeed in that, you have just practiced creative procrastination. It differs from the usual type of procrastination in that it is based on a conscious and rational decision.

To many people, procrastination is a dirty word. But when conscious and creative, procrastination is not a dirty word. It is the ultimate, the Holy Grail of self-management. Why? Because it empowers you to deal with the most rewarding tasks and to *defer* all others.

Procrastination inhibits success only when it deflects you from what you identified as the most important task. Let's say you want to be the primary agent for a 50-dwelling development. You have met the developer and the firm's marketing people. The chemistry is great. The homes are a good value, well built, and the price range is right in your strike zone.

You need to create a plan of attack. If your broker doesn't have a canned presentation—flip charts, slide show, video, whatever—the first step may be to persuade the broker to do his or her part to lock up the deal. Maybe—and it's a big maybe—you can finesse the dog-and-pony show. You have to find out what the developer expects to see and what will sell his or her group on you and your organization.

Perhaps you set a date to introduce the team that will back you up—assuming you have managed to position yourself as the lead agent for the listing. Then you must develop a plan of attack so that everything will be ready on the big day.

That requires a schedule of events, a plan for when the various elements of the plan must be completed. Some elements must be completed before others can start. There are probably mailing lists to compile. You may want to create a special mailing piece. How much promotion is your broker ready to provide, and how will it be invested? You need to plan meetings to discuss the various components of a successful listing and marketing effort.

If you assign top priority to landing this listing, then you allow nothing to interfere with the activities you decide are necessary. When you have created the schedule of events, write them into your planner. They now become your A-1s on the days where you have slotted them.

There may be other As on the page. Tackle them *after* you have fulfilled the requirements of your A-1. If you don't get to them on that day, defer them. You've just procrastinated creatively again.

A Word of Caution

Creative procrastination does not mean the same thing as "consigned to oblivion." It means *deferring* until the most important task is complete. The example above is based on a complex project—signing up a developer—with many parts that must be dealt with sequentially. You'll probably not devote all of each day to them, and that allows you to deal with other—but less—important tasks. Those are A-2s or A-3s.

Maybe you also slotted some Bs on that day. If you don't get to all your As, how are you going to get to the Bs? That's why you only assigned them B priority. Defer them. Creative procrastination can save your life. It can assure your success. It relegates lesser tasks to the future.

Isn't that dangerous? you ask. After all, those B priority tasks were on my to do list. Good question. The answer is that if you call fill your time with A activities, the Bs become less and less important.

Napoleon made a practice, so it is said, never to answer a letter until six months after he received it. His justification came in two parts. The first was that he was busy conquering Europe and a good bit of Africa. That was his *goal*. His other reason is more relevant to our subject: He had learned that most of the problems contained in the letters he received resolved themselves before he got around to opening them. He didn't squander his time solving other people's problems.

This is not suggest that you leave your mail unopened for six months or even six days. It is only to illustrate that refusing to let low-priority tasks interfere with major goals usually has negligible negative consequences and most often confers great rewards. You may not conquer Europe and Africa, but you may very well dominate your little corner of the world.

AVOID TELEPHONITIS AND OTHER INTERRUPTIONS

After your car and your planner, the most important tool you have as a real estate agent is the telephone. It can help expedite, clarify, settle, investigate, inform, remind. It can save you hours and hours every week. Or it can be the biggest time-waster on your desk.

The first thing to remember is that it is a tool, not the boss. It responds to your needs, but has no needs. It has no claim on you or your time. It is there to serve you; you do not serve it.

Obvious, you say. It ought to be, yet many are enslaved by their servant. "I'm expecting a phone call," they say while they sit at their desks waiting for the phone call, which may or may not come. The longer they wait, the more obsessed they become with that phone call. They can't think about anything else, because that phone call has become the most important thing on their minds.

For some people, the sight of a telephone compels them to make a phone call. Or two, or six. If you've ever observed teenagers, you know the disease. The problem is that many of us don't outgrow it.

If you occasionally suffer from compulsive telephonitis, here is a cure. Set aside a specific time of day when you will receive telephone calls. Set aside another time when you initiate or return phone calls. Hohoho, you say. In a real estate office? We live by the telephone! Maybe. And some people die by the telephone.

Let's be practical. Sure. That unexpected phone call may be from the most motivated prospective buyer or lister you'll ever meet. Then again it might not be.

The question is, what are you doing when that phone call comes in? Here you'll see the importance of ganging your phone calls. If you have set aside an hour on this day for prospect calling and an unexpected call comes in, take it. It fits your plan. On the other hand, if you're frantically putting together a tour for Mr. and Mrs. Eager Buyer, stay with your plan. Let someone else tell the caller when you will get back.

And that points up the importance of ganging your outbound calls and setting a time for returning calls. If the person on the desk says to the caller, "Tony Sullivan is showing a property (or on another call or at a closing). Where can you be reached between two and three this afternoon?" The caller will feel that their needs will be attended to. You've risked very little and you have stayed focused on the task you set yourself for this time.

Setting up a system to accomplish this protective device is fairly simple. First, it requires you to set a time when you are available to receive phone calls, and another time when you will return calls. Second, you have to let the people who answer your phone know what your routine is.

If you have a full-time receptionist, give him or her a copy of your daily schedule with your telephone hour(s) highlighted. The person doesn't have to say, "I'm sorry, Ms. Sullivan only accepts phone calls between 10:30 and 11:30." The proper response was given earlier: You are unavailable, but will get back to the person at a specified and suitable time.

If this strikes you as beyond the capabilities of people in your office, you should probably arrange for a telephone trainer to provide instruction in effective telephone technique. Most prospects will appreciate the professional attitude reflected by consideration for their needs. Few will tolerate habitual casualness in returning phone calls, inaccurate messages or, "I don't know when Ms. Sullivan will be back; she didn't leave word."

In Chapter 10, we'll discuss in greater detail how correct telephone procedures save time and sales.

Take Control of Telephone Conversations

If you group your telephone calls, you'll handle them more efficiently for several reasons. First, you will develop a pattern that enables you to state, in the fewest possible words, your business and elicit the information you're looking for. Second, you will minimize the lost motion caused by switching from task to task.

For routine prospecting calls, make a list of the points you want to make. Your goal is to obtain an appointment to visit the property. Develop the shortest route to that goal and follow it. Of course, as in any selling situation, you have to remain flexible. If the prospect indicates an interest in knowing more about you and your agency, show that you're anxious to answer all their questions, but cut to the chase as quickly as possible with, "When would it be convenient for you to show me your house?" The game is played face-to-face.

Few sales are made on the telephone, so if an out-of-town person wants to know all about the community, offer to send a packet of materials on schools, churches, recreational facilities, etc. Be as helpful as you can, within the limits of your available time. Again, drive for the face-to-face meeting. "When do you expect to be in town?" "Can we set up an appointment?"

The purpose here is not to tell you how to sell, but to help you protect your selling time. Lack of discipline in using the telephone can take a large bite out of your production.

Most real estate offices work on the principle that everyone helps everyone else. You cover the phone when your associates are out, and they do the same for you.

Limit your conversation to the essentials suggested above: who; phone number; best time to call. Or, if the associate has a telephone hour, inform the caller when he or she will call back.

If your office doesn't have a code of responsibility to formalize agents' obligations to each other, consider drawing one up. It can prevent ill feelings when someone doesn't protect another's interests, and it can allay suspicion in cases where someone appears to poach or otherwise infringe on your interests. Some ground rules regarding turf and rotation can avoid misunderstandings and the consequent lost time.

Avoiding Other Interruptions

Various studies show that the average executive may deal with as many as 20 different problems an hour and that interruptions come at the rate of every six minutes.

Some have such splendid staff work that they breeze through the day. They have all the information they need at their fingertips to make brilliant decisions. Others get ulcers, kick the dog, scream at the children. All pray fervently for an end to interruptions.

Let's acknowledge that interruptions come in several disguises. There are those we *decree* by insisting on being involved in every decision. Skillful delegation of responsibility and tasks can help resolve those.

There are also those we *create* by interrupting ourselves. We're sailing along when a piece of paper catches our eye, and we decide to work on *it*. Or we suddenly think of a phone call we ought to make—outside of our planned telephone time. The solution is to put all irrelevant paper out of sight and stick to your daily plan. And remember your deadline.

There are those interruptions we *permit* for fear of offending someone. The unannounced visitor, the chatty neighbor at the next desk, the "important" caller with nothing important to say—all team up to squander our valuable time and provide little in return.

If you've kept an accurate time log, you know how much time you spend with casual visitors, those who stop by for a friendly chat on any irrelevant subject. If it amounts to more than a few minutes a day, you're probably wasting more working time than you can afford.

The most direct way to deal with drop-ins is to plead a heavy workload. "I'm getting ready to meet a client, and I have to get this done before I leave," is usually enough to cut the visit to a few seconds.

If the visitor is already in your office (they sometimes arrive when you're out and say, "I'll wait"), ask how you can be of service. If they're only looking for an available ear and yours really isn't, even though you're friends, ask if you can talk about it later—perhaps after your last appointment.

When the visitor has legitimate business but lingers after the business purpose is served, merely standing up is usually enough to signal that the conversation is ending. If it isn't, offer your hand, thank the person for stopping by and promise to get back to him or her while gently urging the visitor toward the door.

Your time log will also show you *who* are the most frequent interrupters. Visitors who take a half-hour to accomplish a one-minute transaction will appear in entries like: "10:45-11:15—Geo M. here, left check." Dropping off a check is serious business, but it doesn't really require 30 minutes of your time.

If Geo M. appears frequently in your time log in the role of a lingerer, you can alert someone in the office to "remind" you of another commitment, say ten minutes after Geo M. arrives. At which point you can excuse yourself.

Another escape is to invite the visitor to accompany you while you walk or drive somewhere to attend to other business. You have legitimized your departure, while offering to listen. When you arrive at your destination, should the visitor have accepted your invitation, thank him or her for accompanying you.

A slightly more difficult situation arises when the visitor has a legitimate business purpose and you have a previous commitment.

Express your pleasure at seeing the visitor and explain that you really do have to run to an appointment. Something like, "Can we talk for five or ten minutes? I'll put together a tour (or whatever is appropriate) and get back to you this afternoon. Can I pick you up somewhere?" will satisfy all but the most impatient prospect. You've shown your interest, demonstrated your desire to help and made a commitment to serve them. And the deadline may just get things done a little faster.

If you sense that the visitor is both serious and impatient, rely on your A-B-C classification. What had you planned for the time slot that is being invaded? Was it A time? What would be the consequences of a postponement? How serious is the visitor?

If postponement would risk a possible sale or listing, and the visitor insists on being served immediately, which is the greater risk? The answer will usually be to sacrifice the drop-in. If the drop-in insists on the right to destroy your plans on the first visit, what special considerations will they demand later on?

Stay Firm but Flexible

The real estate business invites interruptions—both in person and by telephone. Which is why disciplined time management is important; it's a proactive, opportunistic approach to selling. Some people recommend keeping a certain amount of time open in your daily schedule. A better way is to schedule a full day when you can, but know what can be deferred if a potential A shows up.

The time you assigned to make or return phone calls is probably B time. A visitor is potentially A time. Make your decision accordingly.

Skilled use of the telephone coupled with careful planning that keeps your options open are among the best ways to bring your actual time-use performance in line with your ideal allocations so that you achieve all your goals.

CHAPTER 9

What Is Your Time Worth?

You now have set financial goals, tracked your time use for at least two four-week periods and compared your performance with preliminary estimates of the hours you are going to commit to various tasks and to your career.

To overcome any lingering doubts you may still harbor regarding the value of your time, you're now going to calculate the value of your discretionary time in terms of those goals and commitments.

Let's say that you have set $50,000 as your annual income goal. If your company is typical, it offers few if any fringe benefits, so your nominal income is your total compensation. People in other industries performing this calculation may have to add as much as 40 percent to their salary to arrive at their total compensation.

We have also distinguished discretionary time from nondiscretionary time: The first is time spent on tasks that you choose; the second is time over which you have little or no control. Face-to-face activities, the only ones that generate income, usually occur in discretionary time. So do most B activities, those that prepare you for or lead to such opportunities. Nondiscretionary time is taken up with meetings, floor time, writing ads and other C activities, which don't normally produce income.

Therefore, to calculate the value of your time on an hourly basis, you should use only your discretionary time, since that is the only time you can apply to producing income. Most people consider themselves lucky if they can protect 50 percent of their time and use it to pursue their goals. You may have more or less. Your time log and time analysis will have given you a fairly accurate picture of your percentage of discretionary time. Figure out what that percentage is so you can use it in Worksheet 9-1 to calculate the value of your time.

We have gone Benjamin Franklin one better. He said, "Time is money," but he never said how much money. Two dollars? Five dollars? For how much time? Were we supposed to convert all our time to money? That sounds pretty mercenary and dreary.

You now have established the monetary value of your time. The purpose of the exercise is not to puff up your ego or to give you high blood pressure. It is merely to make you aware that based on your goals, commitments and calculations, your discretionary time is worth an astonishing amount. Armed with that knowledge and that awareness, you can now weigh the relative merits of every task you undertake or are asked to undertake.

You should ask yourself, "Why am I doing this?" What goal am I addressing by engaging in this activity? What chance does it have to repay the time investment I am making?

If you can't answer the first or second questions by naming a specific goal, you're probably wasting your time. If you can't answer the third question with confidence that you will be repaid in full, you're working for less than you're worth.

If the answers don't meet these criteria, you may not be able to drop what you're doing immediately, but you can take care not to let the activity drag on or become habitual. It's easy to waste time kaffeklatching, telling war stories, recapping or planning the weekend. Knowing the value of your time gives you the encouragement you need to break away and get on with the day's real work.

EVALUATE THE TIME INVESTED IN MOVING UP

Calculating the value of your time is also useful in planning the investment in time to move into higher-priced properties.

It is impossible to say that X number of hours invested in cultivating an upscale market will result in Y percent larger commissions within a certain period of time. But you can set targets and track your progress. If your average sale is now $100,000, you might say that you

Worksheet 9-1

Value of Time

First calculate the total number of hours you have committed to your work, as follows:

Number of hours committed to real estate
work each week _____

×50 _____

Total number of hours per year _____

Write in the percentage of your total work time you
will apply to income-producing activities. _____ %

Total discretionary time per year _____ hrs

Write in your annual income goal. $ _____

Add the value of your benefits package, if any,
as a percent of your annual income. _____ %

Total value of your benefits package in dollars $ _____

Your total annual compensation $ _____

Divide your total annual compensation by your total annual discretionary time in hours:

$$\frac{\text{total annual compensation}}{\text{total discretionary time}}$$ $ _____

This is the value of one hour of your discretionary time, the time you can apply to achieving your income goals.

As a final exercise, divide the value of one hour of your time by 60 to determine the value of one minute of your time and write on the line below.

One minute of my discretionary time is worth _____ .

want to increase your average to $150,000. Assuming you sell the same number of houses, your commission income will increase 50 percent.

If that increase is, say $10,000 or $25,000, you can easily calculate the amount of time you can economically devote to the effort. Let's say you calculated the value of your discretionary time at $50 an hour. An increase of $10,000 can justify 200 hours. Since you would expect to remain at that new average and probably increase it as you penetrate the high-end market, the investment in time will pay an annual dividend for many years.

Still, 200 hours is a big chunk of time—about four hours a week. However, that's what your planning sessions are for.

Maybe you can't squeeze in four hours a week every week. How about every other week? Instead of reaching that new average in one year, it may take two years.

Again, the important thing is to set the goal, make a plan to achieve it, schedule the activities that will get you there and monitor your progress. You may find yourself approaching your goal faster than planned. If it turns out that way, great; keep up the good work.

If you progress slower than you had anticipated, analyze what you're doing. Are you devoting the time you calculated was required to do the job? What kind of activities are preventing you from devoting the time? Can you adjust your schedule to make the time available?

If you can't make the adjustments in your schedule, you may have to push the horizon out. But whether you achieve your goal later rather than sooner, planning and monitoring will keep you pointed in the right direction and help you determine what corrective actions to take, if any.

The purpose of this exercise, as of all the others, is to help you increase your awareness of how you invest your time and to increase the reward for each hour you spend.

CHAPTER 10

The Time-Managed Office

Time management is a method of focusing on important tasks to achieve personal goals. It is based on setting goals and making plans to achieve them. This requires examining your own priorities, focusing on a few at a time, deferring others and dropping some when their importance diminishes or when they conflict with higher priorities.

And even though most real estate people function as individual entrepreneurs, relying on the fruits of their own efforts, they must also depend on others to achieve their goals.

Not only must they rely on others to answer phone calls, they rely on each other for information, to sit open houses and a host of other tasks that come up at inopportune times.

For this reason, time management is most effective when the entire office is involved. In such an environment, everyone is able to focus on his or her own priorities and still support colleagues' goals. If each person in a group understands that everyone has goals and priorities, which usually come first, conflicts will be more easily resolved.

From the time we developed the ability to express our needs—usually within a few hours after being born and felt the first hunger pang—we became aware that our needs and desires are often in conflict with those of others. No, you can't have your sister's doll. No, you can't have a pony. No, you can't have the car tonight. Sorry, I already have a date for the prom. We can't leave the baby with a sitter when she's teething.

The point is not so much that life is full of little frustrations, but that in order to survive them, we learn to defer, negotiate, compromise and adjust to what others want. So it is with our personal goals and objectives. We create a timetable, list the tasks that must be accomplished by what date in order to achieve them, only to get thrown off-course by an unforeseen event or events. These events usually come in the form of someone else's objectives or priorities. You want to do one thing, and your wife another. The boss reorganizes the office. Your farm is cut in half. Mortgage money dries up as a result of Federal Reserve policy. In some cases, it turns out that one of your goals is an obstacle to achieving your other goals.

The fancy term for this is *priority dissonance*. In everyday words, what you want isn't necessarily what everyone else wants. Your priorities differ from those of people whose support you need.

Time management offers no easy solution to such divergences. What would life be without a few conflicts to keep us awake? On the other hand, when a group of people who must work together find that each is pulling in a different direction, everyone may find they spend an inordinate amount of time on conflict resolution. That isn't even D time!

Time management techniques can, however, help prevent these conflicts before they arise. Although we have described methods of using time effectively, we have really been talking about *management*—mostly *self*-management. Time management is more about management than about time. The ticking of the clock is beyond anyone's ability to manage it. All we can control is how we spend time.

THE MANAGER'S ROLE

The manager must work to obtain maximum effectiveness in the use of *everyone's* time. Again we have a slight misnomer. The ability to manage others is usually more myth than fact. A possible exception is the military, where most orders are self-executing. The general tells the colonel and the colonel tells the major, who tells the captain and so on down the line until it gets to a sergeant who knows which private has the knowledge and energy to perform the task. No questions allowed; no questions asked. No better ways suggested.

In an idealized real world (i.e., a world where companies are run the way everyone agrees companies *should* be run) the role of management is to establish goals and create plans to achieve them.

It is a well-established fact (Tom Peters and his associates have written volumes to document it) that groups work best when they have participated in both setting goals and planning. Having helped build the monster, they now feel some responsibility for mastering it. Management's role then becomes to provide the facilities, capital and human resources to reach those goals.

Peters' thesis is that the people on the firing line know better than anyone what it takes to get a job done—whether it's building better automobiles (Honda) or serving a better hamburger (McDonald's). Management's job is to listen, learn what the staff knows and create realistic corporate goals. Corporate goals thus established are no longer just the boss's goals, but everyone's goals.

Is that the end of the conflict? Will everyone just shrug and smile whenever their personal goals appear to be in conflict with, and obviously must bow to, company goals? That's doubtful. But the mechanism is there—created by all participants—to resolve such conflicts.

Nor does it mean that the mechanism, once created, sits there, like Solomon, with answers for every conflict from now until the end of time. As we stated early on, goals are most useful when they are examined and changed as conditions and people change.

TURNING INDIVIDUAL GOALS INTO COLLECTIVE GOALS

We have suggested several times that individual production goals be set with the advice and consent of the manager. The manager knows what is realistic, given the market, the experience of the individual and other factors that influence performance. The manager also has expectations. Goals must therefore be a joint effort to reflect both sides of the equation and avoid surprises and acrimonious debate.

From individual goals, the manager may establish goals for the brokerage. Notice the direction: office goals are determined by individual goals, not the other way around. Admittedly, if the office is part of a larger network, targets will probably need to be negotiated with headquarters. But the main point is that within the office, individual targets will be shared knowledge, fitting into the office goals, to which each agent contributes.

Keep It Smooth

The manager who helps agents set goals knows how each agent proposes to spend his or her time to achieve those goals. The manager should review each agent's time management plan, again in light of his or her experience, knowledge of the territory and company goals. With this information, the manager is equipped to diagnose shortfalls. Is the person on target? Sticking to plan? This also puts the manager in a position to nudge individuals who are not performing according to their own plans.

The manager who has a copy of each person's plan can make sure that staff is available to perform various office functions. Some managers ask agents to set aside a certain number of hours per week for office functions that may not relate directly to that person's goals. Obviously the time to do this is when discussing that person's goals and plan of action.

Alternatively, the weekly meeting—or some such gathering—is an opportune time to make these time allocations. The guiding principle is "no surprises." An agent won't welcome a surprise announcement that he or she is needed for a special assignment at a time that conflicts with a previously slotted task. Nor does the broker want to hear that no one is available for a task he or she considers important.

As always, anticipation is the key word. A real estate office should only welcome surprises that involve new business. Nothing should be allowed to interfere with opportunity sales, walk-ins and the like. On the other hand, much activity in a real estate office can be anticipated. The better the anticipation, the smoother the operation. And smooth operation usually leads to productivity.

Floor time—keeping the phones covered—is one of the most critical routine tasks in an office. Schedules should be posted as far in advance as possible, ensuring coverage *and* minimum interference with agents' other activities.

Another common office task is attending meetings. Most people agree that meetings are the bane of their existence; so they hold meetings to discuss how to reduce the number and length of meetings. There are no easy solutions; people need to get together. It promotes solidarity and provides an opportunity to buy into company goals. Here are some suggestions to increase meeting effectiveness while decreasing meeting time:

1. Always prepare an agenda and circulate it among those expected to attend. If certain people are to make presentations, make sure they are prepared. Allow people to excuse themselves from meetings if they must be somewhere else. Be sensitive to their needs, while staying alert to the habitual absentee, who always claims, "I have an important appointment at that time."
2. Allocate limited time for each topic to be discussed. Ten minutes is about as long as anyone can stay attentive to one speaker and one topic. Five minutes is better. Two is better still. Psychologists agree that most people's attention spans are limited. You can't beat it, so join it.
3. Avoid pro forma meetings. Hold meetings when they are needed, not because "We always meet at 9:00 every Monday morning." Such meetings almost guarantee half-minded attendance.
4. When you decide to call a meeting, decide who needs to attend as well, and why. Then set a time that is convenient for them. You can do this by circulating a memo stating the purpose of the meeting and asking which of three time slots is most convenient.
5. Allow people to leave when they have contributed all they can. A simple, "I don't think I have anything more to contribute to this meeting," should do it.
6. Have standup meetings. The Japanese use this technique to keep meetings short and to the point.
7. Don't serve refreshments. Some people will stay as long as the refreshments last.
8. Hold meetings before regular working hours. This not only lends an aura of importance, but also reduces interference with the day's work while providing an incentive to stick to the point and come to a decision.
9. Start your meetings on time. And don't repeat anything for the latecomers. Delaying the start or repeating punishes the on-time and rewards the tardy. Habitual late arrivals will get the message after a couple of missed openings.
10. For this reason, prepare your agenda with the most important points first. If this seems harsh on the late arrivals, keep this

equation in mind. The tardy one saves (maybe) the five minutes by which he was late *and costs each of perhaps ten people five minutes—almost an hour of potentially productive time.*

We calculated the value of that time in Chapter 9. A reasonable person will quickly come to the point when reminded that "This meeting is costing about $10 a minute."

WHO'S IN, WHO'S OUT?

This is not about trendiness or the biggest box office draw. It has to do with letting others in on your goings and comings. If the office doesn't have an "in-out" board, someone should dip into the next commission and buy one. Then encourage everyone to use it!

If people are in the habit of grabbing their briefcases and dashing off, it may take some time to get them adjusted to the idea that their whereabouts—or at least their time of reappearance—is important to real estate office operations.

It is a simple matter to create a board with space to list each person's name, followed by a series of boxes. There are innumerable devices, from chalkboards to magnetic and even electronic boards, that allow an agent to check in, or if out, to indicate when he or she will be back. A line to note destination and how to reach the agent is a desirable addition to the basic information.

The time (and commissions!) saved by efficient communications is incalculable. Suffice it to say that one very modest commission will abundantly repay the investment in expediting contact and the ability to say to a caller, "Robin will be back at 3:30. Would you like to leave word?"

AM I MY FILE'S KEEPER?

We'll commit the unpardonable sin of answering a question with a question: If not you, then who?

Anyone who owns two pieces of paper knows that files are desirable. Yet most offices maintain piles instead of files. Something comes into the office, and someone tosses it on top of a pile. The next thing arrives, and it gets tossed onto another pile. Everyone builds and jealously guards his or her own pile. "Don't touch it; I'll never be able to find anything," they howl at the suggestion that their pile is about to topple over.

They waste hours every week looking for things. It's been estimated that the average executive spends as much as three-and-a-half hours a week looking for things. They put things in a safe place "so I'll know exactly where it is when I need it." The place is so safe they can't remember where it is, and the search is on.

If looking for things is an abominable waste of time, it's also a horrendous waste of nervous energy. Is there anything more frustrating than looking for that all-important piece of paper, the one on which you wrote all the options available to finance the ideal house for a prospect who is eager to close? It leaves you exhausted and angry. Or it becomes a preoccupation. I'm going to find it—or else.

Or else, you could reconstruct the puzzle from scratch, but the ideas are never as good as the ones you wrote when you were first inspired by the problem. And it takes time away from other, perhaps more important projects. It cuts into your productive time.

Some of the problems of knowing where you put things will be resolved by using a five-function planner. Your daily activities should all be recorded on the appropriate lines. Notes on conversations, future appointments, important ideas and the like should all be there for instant retrieval whenever and wherever you need them.

Still, there are documents you don't need at your fingertips at all times. Mailing lists, sample advertisements, multilist books, last year's sales figures, all are data that you may want to get your hands on immediately. That's where a reliable filing system is indispensable.

There are innumerable systems on the market to help you organize all those bits of paper. Sometimes you may want to transfer the information to your planner. Many more times, you'll want to tuck it away for future reference.

A simple alphabetical system by topics is easy to start, but it has limitations. First, it's difficult to cross-reference; second, it's easy to outgrow.

Here's an example to illustrate the need for cross-referencing: You might file the Anderson property under "Anderson." But it's in the Fall Creek subdivision, and you're building a reference file of all Fall Creek properties. If you file it under "Fall Creek" and suddenly need to pull up the Anderson property, you'll have to remember that the Anderson property is in the Fall Creek file.

When a file drawer is full and you need to squeeze, say a new Newhart file between Nelson and Nutter, you have to move a lot of bulk.

The solution to both these problems is a numerical system, using an *index* to your files. Let's say Anderson is the first file. You assign number 1 to it, and on the first line of the "A" sheet in your index, you write "Anderson" and the number 1. And you also write "Fall Creek (Anderson)" on the first line of your "F" sheet. Now you'll be able to find it quickly, no matter how you remember it.

You won't have to jam new files between existing ones, because new files are added in sequence. If you have 1001 file folders, the next one will be 1002 and you simply place it in back...carefully noting the contents and number in your index. As your files expand you simply add more file drawer space.

The advantage to such a system is that if you ever need to refer someone to a file when you're out of the office, you just need to tell him or her the file number you want. Or if you leave the index at the office, just give the person the subject.

No one needs to penetrate the mysteries of your "piling" system. All you need to do is show someone your index; he or she will understand exactly how to retrieve the information you're looking for.

SHARE THE NITTY-GRITTY OR ASSIGN IT?

Some real estate offices function well with each agent doing a portion of the no-income chores. Others prefer to hire one person to handle phones, filing and other routine chores, leaving agents free to pursue listings, cultivate prospects and show houses.

Both systems work, but as in any enterprise, the important question is, Can we do it better? Here is a list of questions that will help you determine whether your operation would benefit from having someone take responsibility for the day-to-day office routine.

1. Are telephones fully covered during normal business hours?
2. How many hours does each agent devote to floor time?

3. Does floor time represent a major irritant among agents, an obstacle to meeting sales goals?
4. Are agents keeping individual—and duplicate files—of information that might be better stored in a master file?
5. Is essential information readily available for anyone who needs it?
6. Does someone know at all times where all agents are and their expected times of return?
7. Does everyone know the goals of the office and his or her expected contribution?
8. Do agents feel that office work is interfering with doing their job, which is to sell real estate?
9. Do the forms and reports agents have to submit serve a real purpose? Can they be reduced?
10. Are meetings a forum for an exchange of useful information or are they just a hard-to-break habit?

Giving all the "right" answers to these questions won't solve all the problems that can arise in a real estate office, much less guarantee year after year of spectacular growth. But regular investigations into whether a greater share of time could go into generating commissions will ensure the office is making the best use of its most important resource—the agents' time.

A Word on Delegation

As the boss, you probably have the experience to solve problems more quickly than your associates. And it can be very frustrating to watch someone struggle for days with a problem you could resolve in an hour with a few well-placed phone calls. But learn to stand back. If you make a habit of solving your associates' problems, you may soon find yourself doing little else. And your associates will not develop problem-solving skills they need.

Effective delegation is one of the best ways to acquire time to work on major projects. But it also requires time investment. To be effective, delegation must serve the interests of the person to whom work is being delegated as well as the one doing the delegating.

Here are some questions to ask yourself when delegating a task:

- Why am I delegating this task?
- What will I do with the time gained by delegating it?
- Is the person capable of carrying out the assignment?
- Have I given clear instructions?
- Does the person understand exactly what I expect?
- Have I tried to delegate a task or a responsibility?
- What will the person learn from performing this task?

If your answers suggest you're delegating a task that you feel is boring or presents a high probability of failure, or for which you haven't taken the time to make clear your expectations, or that will not help the person learn a useful skill, the risk may be greater than the few minutes of time you gain.

TOOLS OF THE TRADE

There are many gadgets on the market these days that can support your efforts to provide the best service to your clients and prospects—the kind of service that brings referrals from people you have served well in the past.

We have already discussed the importance of a planner that incorporates the five functions of an effective time management system. It is indispensable, for it provides a single place to record all the important information that relates to your work.

As has been said millions of times in a different context, "Never leave home without it." In fact, many successful agents never go *anywhere* without their planners. It's on the night table when they go to bed; it's in front of them at their desks, on the seat beside them in the cars, at their elbow during any discussion. If it seems out of place anywhere, at least have some punched sheets to jot down any ideas so you can then insert them in your planner later.

We repeat again that a minute spent planning a job saves three minutes in doing the job. A real estate agent's life is filled with minutes of waiting that can be put to good use—if you have your planner at hand to jog your memory or to receive those sudden inspirations that can close a deal.

Car Phone or Pager?

Most agents spend a large part of their day outside of the office. It's not that difficult to stay in touch; you're never far from a telephone.

On the other hand, if an important call comes for you at the office, it may be advantageous to respond before your hourly call in. A pager can alert you to an incoming call and tell you who's calling and where that person can be reached.

A car phone is a bigger investment with bigger benefits. It allows you to put driving time to constructive use. If you set a time when you return calls, you don't have to stay at the office to do it; you can be on your way to an appointment. If you're meeting someone and have to wait, you can catch up on your phone calls. If you're going to be late, you can call ahead and explain without having to make yourself even later by watching for the next service station with a phone booth—where three truck drivers are waiting to use it. And you're always reachable.

Twenty-Four-Hour Coverage of Your Telephone

Some people hate them while others say they couldn't live without them. Answering machines can be useful in a brokerage office, even one with carefully planned telephone procedures.

Clients can't always be counted on to respect your posted office hours. If they call when you're closed or, heaven forbid, if everyone is out, your machine can tell them when you'll be back.

If you publish your home phone number, which most real estate agents do, an answering machine can reassure callers that you'll get back to them.

If you have a private number at your office, an answering machine can protect your telephone hours. Your message can say, "Terry Blandon can't come to the phone right now, but if you leave your name and number, he will call you back at 3:15 today." If you're in the office, you may choose to take the call then. Either way it helps put you in control.

Three things to remember regarding answering machines: First, you have to turn it on. Second, you have to check it for messages. And third, it's a business tool and should not be confused with the microphone at the local comedy club.

Measuring Devices

Every real estate person feels a tingle when the client starts mentally placing the furniture in the house you're showing: "Let's see, how long is this room? I wonder whether our living room rug will fit."

That's when you whip your little sonic "measuring stick," aim it, press the button and presto, you can give the client the exact length and width. It beats getting on your hands and knees (and sometimes asking the client to do the same!) if you or the client don't want to depend on the dimensions given on the listing sheet.

It's a useful gadget when listing a property, too, because it can save much of the time it takes to measure each room, to say nothing of snagged stockings and soiled trouser knees.

More Than Just a Calculator

Some calculators answer many questions clients ask that others can't. Sure, with your interest-table book and a ten-dollar calculator you can tell what the monthly payment is on a 30-year mortgage at $10^1/_2$ percent. "But what will my equity be after five years?" your client might ask. Or how much faster would I build up equity if I pay an extra ten dollars a month? Or if I round it off the next highest hundred each month?

An only slightly more sophisticated financial calculator can give you the answer in seconds. Yes, it may take an hour or so to learn the keystrokes, but it can help you give your clients essential information that can lead to a quicker decision and an earlier closing.

Is There a Computer in the House?

Although computers are common in real estate offices, many people retain a strong aversion to them. Computer phobia, resistance to change, expense, lack of space and unperceived need are but a few of the reasons. Whatever the reason, reviewing the computer's advantages in terms of time management could pay substantial dividends.

If the multilist in your area is computerized, you can save valuable hours every time you put together a tour. Instead of leafing through a book, you can punch in various criteria, such as price and location, and the computer will show you a list of properties that meet those requirements.

If you send out mailings, the computer will not only maintain your lists, it also will print out address labels and personalized letters.

If you deal in investment properties, a computer can calculate internal rates of return and other essentials on which to base buying decisions.

And that just scratches the surface of computer capabilities. A computer can store literally tons of information on a few disks. It can organize the information so that desired information is on your desk in seconds. It can crunch numbers a thousand times faster than the best calculator. With a simple add-on called a modem (modulator-demodulator), it can talk to other computers and receive information from them.

And learning to use a computer isn't all that difficult. Graybeards and five-year-olds become computer literate with astonishing ease using today's user-friendly machines. Taking the time to acquire basic computer skills will repay you handsomely.

Once you get acquainted, you'll find hundreds of additional uses—from taxes to payroll. Stay in touch with your local vendor to keep abreast of new programs that increase the usefulness of your computer and help you use your time more efficiently.

Many state boards have centrally located mainframe computers connected to terminals in brokerage offices throughout the state. Using the keyboard and the modem, agents can access local listings and demand information such as amortization schedules. The programs are installed in the mainframe, but the information is printed out in their own offices.

Let Your Fax Do the Walking

That symbol of life in the fast lane, the fax, can speed printed information across the city or around the globe in a few minutes.

If you need some important details, such as floor plans, from the listing agent on a property you've shown, they can be in your hands in minutes. And you don't have to make a special trip to pick them up.

If both you and your out-of-town client have access to fax machines, you can send copies of new listings as soon as they come in. And if they decide to buy, you can pass most of the documents back and forth on your fax. Only the required "wet" copies need to be physically transferred.

Analyze your needs before you make the plunge. The price range of fax machines can be daunting, but they can save a busy brokerage hours of time and miles of driving, while helping to expedite transactions.

Using Travel Time Constructively

Most modern cars include a tape deck. You can use it play your favorite pop or classical audiotapes. Or you can use it to advance your career by increasing your knowledge.

Hundreds of audiocassettes offer training in everything from foreign languages to relieving stress, from negotiating skills to finance. Your car's tape deck can turn otherwise unproductive—and boring—travel time into a career enhancement opportunity.

A hand-held tape recorder can be another time-saving tool. You can use it to record on-the-spot impressions of clients, prospects and properties. On a caravan, you can "jot down" any prospects who might be interested in any property you see. Or, use it to "write" letters that can be transcribed by someone else when you get back to the office.

Sporting Goods

One successful agent said, "My golf clubs are the most valuable selling tool I have. I do more business on the golf course than in the office." He happens to work for a large organization that develops golf communities. His ability to demonstrate the benefits—while subtly nudging the prospect to a decision—gives him a tremendous advantage. He doesn't have to play the round, but he has the option.

Tennis racquets serve the same purpose, even though it's not as easy to press your advantage during a tennis match. The competition is a little more personal, more like hand-to-hand combat. But the point is the same: *Optimum homophily.* People prefer to do business with people that resemble them—in their tastes, language, sports. Shared interests can help reduce the time required to establish you as "my kind of person, the kind I like to deal with."

Needless to say, however, if you're the club champ, it might be wise to be your client's partner rather than his or her opponent.

CHAPTER 11

The Life Cycle of a Real Estate Agent

Early in this book, we nodded to the inevitable truth that times change, circumstances change and we change. All those changes pose new challenges and opportunities. In Chinese, the word *crisis* also means opportunity.

Let's start with changes in ourselves. Needs that we once classified as necessities fade into the merely desirable or even trivial. Or we may have fulfilled the need. In either case, they don't engage our attention to the same degree as they once did. Which is why goals should be written. In writing, they can be examined and re-evaluated, a very different thing from forgetting, the frequent fate of unwritten goals.

Such examinations and re-evaluations are critical to effective time management in any field, particularly the real estate business, where success depends on individual effort. Even as a member of a multi-office organization with bases in several states, each person is an entrepreneur. Within certain limits, agents set their own pace, decide where to concentrate their efforts, take responsibility for developing networks that generate referrals, enroll in courses that will enhance their skills, even decide to read a book that will develop the time management skills to help them identify and accomplish their lifetime goals.

Entrepreneurs are blessed with vision and drive. They recognize an opportunity where others see nothing. They can pour all their energy into developing it—to a point. For hidden in that blessing is also a curse: The ability to focus all that energy and single-mindedly pursue that vision is frequently accompanied by a need to have their hands on all the levers.

If the market should suddenly change, they may not notice it until it's too late. They didn't notice the changing environment, and they had no confidence in anyone's judgment but their own. The needs they were so good at meeting no longer exist, and someone else has jumped on the new opportunity.

PRIMARY NEEDS AND TASKS CHANGE WITH EXPERIENCE

As a newcomer to the real estate business, your principal concern was to develop a prospect list. What houses can I list? Where are the people who are going to buy? In an established brokerage, the phone will ring, and you may or may not get a share of that business. But if you only wait for the phone to ring, you may have a long wait.

So you call—in person or by phone. You write cards. You offer to provide a market price for likely targets who are not on the market. You keep busy performing professional services with payoffs that are often far, far in the future.

And you arrange your discretionary time to concentrate on those activities, even though you know they won't yield immediate rewards. But what choice do you have? You're paying your dues: cold-calling, doing floor time, knocking on doors, knocking yourself out, reminding yourself that someday all this will pay off.

Sure enough, your efforts eventually begin to produce results. Those hundred calls produce a listing, and you have a project to nurture. That listing won't produce a commission until it's sold. So you make a subtle shift in your time allocation to serve that listing. You have ads to write. You'll probably want to let other agents know about your listing. You need to plan an open house.

Obviously, you're not going to rewrite your whole routine to serve one listing. That's why we say a *subtle* shift. On the basis of the calculated value of your time, you can say that a particular listing merits a certain number of hours of your time.

Let's say it's a $100,000 listing with a 6 percent commission, which you expect to be divided between the listing and selling broker. If your broker splits commissions 50–50 with agents, your share is $1,500. Now divide that by the hourly value of your discretionary time (Chapter 9) by, say, $30 an hour. That commission is worth 50 hours of your discretionary time.

In a hot market, your listing may sell within a week, before you even spend five hours serving it. Or, as you're putting up the sign, someone stops, makes an appointment and makes a full-price offer the next day—through you! You're a double winner, collecting both a listing and a seller's commission with a day-old listing.

On the other hand, the listing may languish. It's not in the most desirable neighborhood. The open house was a bust. The owners move out, so the house doesn't show that well. Two months later, it's still sitting there. You persuade the owner to drop the price 10 percent. A month later, you get an offer—through another agent—that's another 10 percent below the new listed price. Your $3,000 commission just shrank to $1,200.

NOT ALL PROSPECTS ARE CREATED EQUAL

Everyone would like to have more prospects on the verge of buying or selling, who say their needs are urgent and really mean it! Unfortunately, they're usually a small percentage. Many more are looking for "just the right house," which may mean anything from idle curiosity to "I'll know it when I see it." You probably learned to tell the difference as soon as you were exposed to the various types. Conventional wisdom would say to focus on those who are really ready to buy and keep in touch with the others without wasting too much time.

That's fair enough—as far as it goes. But when your prospect list is short, as it's apt to be when starting out, you have the time to turn idle curiosity into effective curiosity and eventually into real interest in a specific property.

Again, there is no intention to get into selling techniques. The point is that if you can't fill your A time target, drop back to B or even C. If, for whatever reason, you can't meet face-to-face with *serious* buyers, try using the time to convert less-than-serious buyers into hot prospects.

For instance, if you've been showing houses to a couple for six months, you probably know the features that appeal to them and those that are turn-offs. Maybe it's time to call the elderly couple who spoke vaguely of moving to Florida "some day." They may be moved to action when they meet the couple that has been wanting that particular neighborhood all along.

The moral is this: The value of your time changes with circumstances. Time management seeks to maximize the return on each unit of time. But on occasion we have to "submaximize." Even though you have calculated the value of your discretionary time at $50 an hour, there are times when $40 is all there is. Take it with a smile and keep pushing.

MAKE A COMMITMENT TO SELLING IT FAST

It's a well-known fact in real estate that prices weaken with time. In a lively market, a property can often bring in more than the asking price if it sells during the first week or so it's on the market. After a month, the chance of getting the full asking price is about even. After that, the property is old news, and the selling price is apt to shrink accordingly.

The lesson is obvious: you get a bigger dividend on the time you invest in selling a property the first week than a month later. Most agents know that subconsciously. After a few weeks, they lose interest in the property. Some firms promise to advertise a property until it's sold, which maintains a degree of awareness both among agents and prospective buyers. After two or three months, though, it may raise some embarrassing questions: What's wrong with it? Is it overpriced? Is the neighborhood deteriorating?

If a house doesn't sell within the average time for properties in its price range, the price certainly needs to be looked at. Was the price set too high at the outset? Did the agent agree to the seller's inflated valuation?

Some agents who agree to put a house on the market at the owners' price do so only with the understanding that they will lower the price by a certain amount within a set period of time *and leave it with the original listing agent.*

While this seems to describe the life cycle of a listing more than of an agent (and also creeps into the area of selling), there are connections between the two.

STARTING OUT

As we have noted, a new associate usually has a good deal of groundwork to do before his or her efforts begin generating a steady income stream. One reason is that new agents have less discretionary time to devote to activities that produce commissions.

Frequently, they don't have the connections and entrés that enable them to apply much of their time to those activities. And they may not have access to the higher-priced properties that produce correspondingly fat commissions.

Working a farm frequently develops contacts. Properly done, farming is an organized and systematic form of cold-calling. After several visits to the same homes and owners, it loses some of the negative aspects of cold-calling, but you're still talking to people whose needs and intentions are not clear. The payoff is slow, yet some successful agents work their farms for years with gratifying results.

The point is that a new agent will probably have to spend a disproportionate amount of time at tasks that have either low hourly payout or a very long-range payoff.

If, on the other hand, you are well known in the community, know the movers and shakers, those who are moving up or out and can translate social contacts into business relationships, you may very well be able to concentrate your discretionary time on income-generating activities early in your career.

Service Wins the Day

Let's repeat the phrase we borrowed from Don Wilson, one of the most successful seminar leaders on selling: *Optimum homophily.* People like to do business with people they're comfortable with. What makes them comfortable? Realizing that they share interests and backgrounds.

Many paths can lead to establishing shared feelings and interests. Simplistically, we might say that men talk about sports and women talk about children. But it isn't that simple. Some men hate sports; not all women have or want children.

When these bridges don't exist, one common interest remains: service. Everyone appreciates service. Some people demand it and make their demands explicit. When cut to a $450,000 monthly allowance,

Donald Trump observed that rich people don't want to wait for anything. In real estate, people have to wait—for the right house, for the right buyer, for the mortgage approval. And the agent shares the waiting. Does time management offer any insights or remedy? Can waiting and efficient use of time be reconciled?

We have already discussed waiting for clients to show them houses and ways to make use of that time. The inevitable waiting between events leading up to a closing calls for a different strategy, one that will vary among agents, market conditions and locations. And each individual's concept of service can influence that strategy.

A now legendary real estate agent, Olivia Hsu Decker, had trouble breaking into the business because of her ethnic background. When a broker gave her a chance, she burned up the track, leading the office in her first year. In 1987, she sold $33 million, making her the top Merrill Lynch luxury-home agent in the country.

What insights we have into Ms. Decker's time management techniques suggests they are not for everyone. She normally works a ten- to twelve-hour day and a seven-day week. What is significant is that she arranges for garbage pickup, phone service and such other above-and-beyond courtesies as finding a decorator and helping to rent the old house until it is sold.

Working in the luxury home market certainly helps to achieve eight-figure sales, and five-figure commissions justify extraordinary effort. How, you may ask, can I spend time on what we agree are C activities when my commission may only be a few hundred dollars?

This is a good question, and one for which we can only provide guidelines to help individuals find their own answer.

What Does Your Traffic Bear?

A similar success story occurred in the Northeast, where a Korean-American agent had trouble, first, finding employment and second, getting started once she was hired.

She achieved success when she recognized her Korean background as an asset. She created a network among her Korean-American friends and created a "niche" for herself. The houses she listed and sold were not in the upscale neighborhoods, but there were enough of them to provide her with a very nice income.

Which brings us back to our friend, optimum homophily. While on the West Coast, Ms. Decker first had to overcome resistance to background; the agent on the East Coast made it an asset. She could not afford to provide extraordinary service—*except by local standards.* She gave her Korean clients better service than they were accustomed to and gained their loyalty.

There is no easy formula to apportion time between earning commissions for today and laying the groundwork for next year's commissions. Sometimes they go hand in hand; a sale on or near the asking price and an orderly closing helps build your reputation for good solid work.

Moving up into the next quality tier and price of homes may require something more. An investment of time to provide truly memorable service is a way that many have used successfully. Again, time must be allocated in a systematic way so that it becomes a part of your career-building program.

Your geographical area and your assigned share of it will, to a large extent, suggest the activities and connections that will help you move from one price level to another. Once you identify them, make them part of your daily planning so that you keep working toward your objective. Allow time to provide memorable service and devise means to remind people of the service you provided. Ms. Decker throws parties for her clients in her own home.

This does not contradict all we have said about the need to focus on income-producing activities. On the contrary, it points up the need to invest time to steer your career to the destination you select.

If you have no luxurious home in which to throw lavish parties, perhaps you have a backyard grill. That's what another successful agent does, explaining that she uses D time (nonwork time and activities) to produce face-to-face situations—A time. The service skills you develop can become your most effective tools of the trade.

Professional Development

Although a new agent may enjoy less discretionary time than a veteran, certain activities should be assigned high priorities. This means you must make time for them.

If you intend to make real estate a lifetime career, you should probably consider further academic training. The time commitment may be intimidating, but through time management you can find it—by learning to use scraps of time. For instance, you can study for advanced real estate or management courses when you're doing floor time; you can take professional journals with you when meeting a prospect; and you can keep a stack of instructional audiocassettes on hand to listen to while traveling or waiting for your prospect.

Although many demands are made on your time, the "do it now" advice applies to increasing your academic knowledge in the early years of your career. You'll have even less time as you incur other obligations. And you'll be reluctant—quite rightly—to put books ahead of prospects. Use your daily planner to block out classroom and preparation time, so that you meet all your commitments.

Delegation

At some point in their careers, many successful real estate people have said something like, "I have so much to do I wish I were twins." A more practical approach is judicious and skillful delegation.

Except for the broker or manager, the real estate office is usually a community of equals. While seniority and productivity may earn special privileges—often unstated but nonetheless real—more favors are granted and more services are exchanged through negotiation and persuasion than by direct orders. Delegation, the method by which busy executives supposedly shed routine tasks to focus on corporate objectives, is not readily available in most real estate offices.

However, there are opportunities. Many offices assign new associates to work with veterans so they may learn the ropes, develop "people" skills, adapt to the company culture and generally get properly launched on their new career.

If you are the "greenie" assigned to an old pro, treat it as invaluable training that can save you a lot of time. You'll learn procedures and methods that produce results. You'll learn about conditions and practices that are peculiar to your market. And you will probably meet people who will be important to you in your work—mortgage lenders, title companies, appraisers, other agents, etc.—while developing your outside contacts in the market.

If, on the other hand, you are asked to help get a new associate started, you can adjust your schedule to include more face-to-face activities. Here is some of the routine work you can hand over to a new associate:

1. Telephone calls. Not every call needs your undivided attention. As soon as you determine the caller's purpose, say, "I'm glad you called. I'm going to ask my associate Lee to get on the phone with us. She is very familiar with that situation and can handle it very well for you." Of course, you need to make sure that Lee is in fact very familiar with that situation.

    That illustrates the point that delegating requires a certain amount of effort on your part. You need to let the person know what you want done, when you want it done, and how much discretion he or she has in executing the assignment. The associate should also understand what you expect by way of reports: daily, weekly, oral, written, or only if there are problems.
2. Meetings. If you have the option, let your colleague attend meetings to which you have little to contribute and from which you expect little benefit.
3. Computer scans. Putting together a list of properties for a prospective buyer can be time-consuming, but it also is an opportunity to become familiar with the market. This can make such work a valuable part of a new agent's training.

The art of effective delegation is one well worth cultivating. While delegating may actually *increase* demands on your time, look on it as an investment. Used with understanding and appreciation of its limits, it is potentially one of the most important and effective time management techniques. When used to unload boring or risky tasks onto others, it can be the greatest source of tension and resentment in any office.

We discuss delegation here because it plays a vital part in the life cycle of a real estate agent whose skills in meeting buyer needs are in such demand that he or she can focus time and energy on only the most rewarding aspects of the profession.

As Robert Dorney said, "The only reason for time management is to get the things you don't enjoy doing out of the way so you can get on with those you really enjoy." We can paraphrase that to say that time management means reducing the time we spend on the least rewarding activities so that we can focus on the most rewarding ones.

In any endeavor, the most successful people are those who understand the value of their time and "sell" it for the highest possible price.

Appendix

Following is a partial list of manufacturers and distributors with a brief description of their product lines. No judgment is offered regarding their relative merits. All are widely used by thousands of successful people, most of whom are persuaded that the system they use is the best.

The perception of value also is highly subjective. Complete systems may be purchased for less than $30 and prove useful to their owners. Other systems offer exotic leather binders, which their advocates feel are indispensable—either to convey a certain image or to indulge their love of luxury.

Readers are encouraged to investigate the products of various manufacturers by catalog and decide which system can best fulfill their time management needs. Because prices may change from year to year, they are not included here; current prices are best obtained directly from manufacturers.

- *Day Runner*—Offers both $5^{1}/_{2}'' \times 8^{1}/_{2}''$ and $3^{3}/_{4}'' \times 6^{3}/_{4}''$ pages. Monthly pages are dated; daily calendar pages are not. Sold through retail outlets and by direct mail. Harper House, Inc., 3562 Eastham Drive, Culver City, CA 90232. 800-635-5544.
- *Day-Timers, Inc.*—The system used in the various examples in this book. Offers several desk and pocket sizes, wire-bound or in ring binders. Basic system can be individualized with more than 50 dif-

ferent auxiliary forms. One Day-Timer Plaza, Allentown, PA 18195-1551. 215-395-5889.
- *FiloFax*—Wide range of sizes and prices reflecting emphasis on luxury leathers. Offers forms to track virtually any activity. Sold principally through upscale retail outlets. 500 West Avenue, Stamford, CT 06902-6325. 800-345-6798. Can be ordered through 800-YESFILL.
- *Franklin International Institute*—Offers two sizes of kit: $5^{1}/_{2}'' \times 8^{1}/_{2}''$ and $8^{1}/_{2}'' \times 11''$, both of which include a selection of forms in a binder. Customer may order forms separately to suit individual needs. P.O. Box 31406, Salt Lake City, UT 84131-0406. 800-654-1776.
- *MoreTime*—A $5^{1}/_{2}'' \times 8^{1}/_{2}''$ system consisting of weekly/daily schedule and planning pages, note pages and checklists, all of which are ordered individually for insertion in a three-ring binder. Order Department, 240 Portland Avenue, Minneapolis, MN 55415. 800-328-0324.
- *Realtimer*—Sold through Roger Butcher Seminars, which are seminars for real estate professionals. The $5^{1}/_{2}'' \times 8^{1}/_{2}''$ pages are available in weekly and daily formats in either leather or vinyl binders. 1808 Tribute Road, Suite B, Sacramento, CA 95815. 800-927-5115.
- *Time/Design*—A comprehensive system in a $5^{3}/_{4}'' \times 8^{1}/_{2}''$ format based on dated daily, weekly and monthly pages. Focus is on project management with more than 50 additional forms and accessories for special needs. 11835 Olympic Blvd., Los Angeles, CA 90064. 800-637-9942.
- *Time/Systems*—Both $5^{1}/_{2}'' \times 8^{1}/_{2}''$ and $8^{1}/_{2}'' \times 11''$ systems consist of dated monthly pages and undated calendar pages. Sold by direct mail or at company headquarters. Half-day training sessions at buyers' offices can be arranged. 5353 N. 16th St., Suite 400, Phoenix, AZ 85016.

Bibliography

Allen, Jane Elizabeth. *Beyond Time Management.* Reading, Mass.: Addison-Wesley, 1986. Discusses the need for organizational systems and goals to be understood by those who must live with and achieve them.

Bliss, Edwin C. *Getting Things Done.* New York: Scribner's, 1976. A collection of brief essays on dealing with specific tasks and problems such as correspondence, indecision, bottlenecks, commuting, etc., as well as obstacles to productivity, such as meetings.

DiAntonio, Steve. *Making Time: The Resourceful Woman's Guide to Delegating Household Tasks.* New York: Ballantine, 1986. How a career woman can avoid having a second full-time career managing a home by delegating and hiring outside help to gain time for enjoyment.

Hobbs, Charles R. *Time Power.* New York: Harper & Row, 1987. The process of time management begins with "unifying principles," which are each person's basic value system. Achievement is enhanced when performance and principles are "congruent."

Kaufman, Phyllis C., and Arnold Corrigan. *How to Use Your Time Wisely.* Stamford, Conn., 1987. An elaboration of the GOLD principle—setting Goals, Organizing your priorities, Listing tasks and Doing it now.

MacKenzie, R. Alec. *Time for Success: A Goal Setter's Strategy.* New York: McGraw-Hill, 1989.

MacKenzie, R. Alec. *The Time Trap: The New Version of the 20-Year Classic on Time Management.* New York: AMACOM, 1990. Based on the author's experience helping top managers deal with inevitable interruptions. Tips on delegating, making decisions and overcoming procrastination.

Moscowitz, Robert. *How to Organize Your Work and Your Life.* Garden City, N.Y.: Doubleday & Co., 1981. How to set goals, establish priorities and meet your deadlines. Suggestions for using odd moments and places to work. Programs for lawyers, doctors and other professionals.

Oncken, William, Jr. *Managing Management Time: Who's Got the Monkey?* Englewood Cliffs, N.J.: Prentice-Hall, 1984. How the organization wastes time and inhibits productivity by creating tasks that have little if anything to do with the organization's goals. The author's "monkey analogy" is legendary in management circles.

Schlenger, Sunny, and Roberta Roesch. *How to be Organized in Spite of Yourself.* New York: New American Library, 1989. No matter what kind of person you are, you can make better use of your time and your space without violating your basic personality.

Shook, Robert L. *Real Estate People.* New York: Harper & Row, 1980. Brief profiles of successful real estate people—their goals, methods and approaches to their careers.

Index

A

ABC of time management, 8, 46, 67, 82
Academic training, 133–34
Accelerating change, 11
Activities
    face-to-face, 109
    listed, 84–85
    value of, 13
Adjustment
    of goals, 53
    of priorities, 114
    time-use, 86–89
Agreement to closing schedule, 71
Analysis, time-use, 85–89
Answering machine, 50, 123
Anticipation, 116
Appointment book, 56
Appointments with yourself, viii, 70, 73
Attention span, 117
Audiocassettes, 126, 134

B

Balance
    in life, 25
    search for, 6
Behavior, influenced by goals, 15
Benefits, 109
Boring tasks, 98
"Bottom feeder," 19
Business, as an excuse, 98

C

Calculator, 124
Career goals, 36
Car phone, 123
Categories, detailed, 87–88
Change, acceleration of, 11

Cold calls, 10
"Command performance," 47, 65, 76
Commitment
    power of, 69
    re-evaluating, 93
    time, 47
Community responsibilities, 43–44
Complacency, 24
Compromise, 114
Computer, 124
Confidence, gaining from goals, 34
Conflict, 113–15
Connections, 131
Control, 1–3
    achieving, 95
    of discretionary time, 56
    of events, 5, 13
    of power, 14
    of telephone calls, 105
Corrective action, 112
Couples, 73–74
Cross-reference, 119

D

Daily action plan, 24
Daily planning session, 52, 66–67
Day-Timers, Inc., 57, 137
Deadline, 30, 100, 101
Decisions, 2, 76, 102
Deferring, 103, 114
Delegation, 102–3, 121–22, 134–35
    upward, 79
Development, professional, 133
Diary and work record, 70, 75, 82–83
Dilemmas, 76
Discretionary time, 7, 56, 65–67, 109–10, 131
Distractions, 96
Distribution, time-use, 86–87
Do it now, 97, 134

141

Dreams
    converted to goals, 29
    differ from goals, 16
Driving time, 123
Drop-ins, 107–8
Dues, paying, 65, 128

E

80-20 trap, 81
Emulation, 19
Entrepreneur, 113, 127
Estimates, of time, 100
Evaluation, 84–85
Events
    control of, 5, 13
    schedule of, 102
Examination of goals, 127
Expectations, 101, 122
Expense record, 57
Experience, 128–29

F

Face-to-face activities, 51, 109
Failure, fear of, 98
Family responsibilities, 42–43
Farming, 19
Favors, earning, 65
Fax, 125
$15 phone call, 10
Files, 118–20
Flexibility, 105
    vs. firmness, 108
    in goals, 33
Floor time, 120
Follow-up, 75
Forgetting, 98
Frustration, 114

G–H

Game plan, 78
Ganging, 104
Goals, 66
    addressing specific, 70
    adjusting, 53
    collective, 115–16
    conflicting, 35, 113
    congruent with values, 33
    converted into action, 29, 35–36
    criteria for, 29–31
    defining, 29–31
    effect on others, 41
    five-year, 25–27
    immediate, intermediate,
        long-term, 32
    importance of written, 33
    income, 9
    influence on behavior, 15
    life, 13–17
    need to change, 34
    of others, 113
    one-year, 17–21
    power of, 14
    professional, 36, 89
    review and update of, 73
    time management, 101
    translated into tasks, 31
    translated to commissions, 37–39
Gossip, 2
Grouping activities, 63, 70
Guidelines, 48
Guilt feelings, xiv
Habits, 24, 95
High producers, 7

I–J

Ideal, achieving your, 89, 93
Imagination, 18–19
Important versus urgent, defined, 49–50
Income, 22, 86
Income target, 89
Information, value of, 9
In-out board, 118
Intention, vague, 69
Interruptions, xiv, 1, 84, 97, 103–4
    sources of, 106–8
Investment
    of time, 137
    properties, 125
Job description, 44

L

Life cycle
    of listing, 130
    real estate agent, 11, 127–29
Life plan, 20
Listing follow-up, 71
Listings, 9
List, prospect, 128
Luxury home market, 132

M

Mailing lists, 125
Master file, 120

Index

Measuring tool, 124
Meetings, 76, 116–18, 135
Memory, 84
Meshing, 71
Milestones, 32
Mind dump, 49, 51, 67
Moving up, 110, 112

N

Necessities, 127
Needs, primary, 128–30
Negotiation, 114, 42
Networks, 127, 132
No
    saying, 77
    when boss must say, 79
Nondiscretionary time, 7, 47–48, 65–66, 109
Numerical system, of filing, 120

O

Obligations
    agent-to-agent, 106
    inventory of, 44
Obsession, 104
Office system, meshing with, 71–73
Office, time-managed, 113–15
Open houses, 77
Opportunities, 77
Opportunity sales, 116, 126
Options, 76

P–Q

Pager, 123
Parkinson's Law, 99–100
Participation, 115
People pleasers, 78
People responsibilities, 41–42
People skills, 134
Performance, matching to goals, 81–83
Performance target, 37
Phone record sheet, 70
Plan
    daily action, 24
    of attack, 102
Planner, 119
    illustrations, 58–60
Planning, 50, 65–67, 98
    daily session, 52
Playing office, 86
Postponement, 108
Power, control of, 14

Power of goals, 14
Preoccupation, 119
Priorities, xiii, 9, 47, 58–60, 67, 95
    setting, 51
Priority dissonance, 114
Problems
    defining, 20
    of others, 103
Procrastination, xiv, 1, 23, 97–99
    creative, 102
Productivity, 2
Professional development, 8, 133
Professionalism, measuring level of, viii
Prospecting, 47
Prospects, 129
Quotas, 29

R

Rational decision, 102
Real estate agent
    as matchmaker, xii
    average earnings of, xii
    life cycle of, 11, 129–31
Real estate tasks, 45
Realism in goals, 23–24
"Real time," 82
Receptionist, 105
Re-evaluation, 127
Referrals, 72
Reports, 135
Reschedule, 100
Resentment, 135
Responsibilities, xii–xiii
    code of, 106
    defining, 41–43
    task, 41
Retirement plan, 22
Review, manager's, 116
Risk, minimizing, 78–79
Role
    front-line, 79
    of manager, 114–15
    staff, 79
Role models, 18
Rollover, of schedule, 75
Routine, 6
    office, 120–22

S

Sales meetings, 77
Schedule

of events, 102
flexibility of, 2
Scheduled activities, 67
Scheduling, 44
Self-interest, 78
Self-management 2, 81
Selling time, protection of, 106
Service, 128, 131–32
Shifts
    macro, 87
    in time allocation, 128–29
    upward, 88
"Significant few," 81
Skills, 99
    people, 136
    problem-solving, 121
Slots, open, 72–73
Social contacts, 131
Stand-up meetings, 117
Starting out, 131
Stress, 100
Stressless home, 42
Stretch factor, 30
Subordinates, 79
Success, 56
Surprises, 77, 116
System
    creating a, 55–57
    personal productivity, 57

T

Tape recorder, 126
Target dates, 31
Tasks
    classification of, 46
    components of, 99–100
    responsibilities, 41
    unfamiliar, 98
Telephone, 50, 120
    calls, 135
    coverage, 123
    $15 call, 10
    log, illustration, 61
    trainer, 105
Telephonitis, 103–4
Tension, 78, 135
Thieves of time, 63
Tickler-reminder, 57
Time analysis form, illustrations, 88–90
Time
    allocation by responsibility, 45–46
    allocation, formula for, xiii

analysis, sheets, 90–92
as resource, 2
defined, 20
discretionary, defined, 7, 65
estimates, 43, 100
frame, 18
insufficient, 98
investment of, 133
log, 56, 78, 83, 97, 107
nondiscretionary, defined, 7, 65
scraps of, 72–73
segments, 82
setting limits, 23
travel, 126
unproductive, ix
value of, 11, 109–11
wasters, 2, 78, 86, 104
Time-managed office, 113–15
Time management
    ABC of, 8, 46, 67, 82
    defined, 5
    goals, 101
Time target, 129
Timetable, 73, 100
To do list, viii, 48, 56, 67, 69, 75
Tools of the trade, 122
Transaction, viii, 52
Travel time, 63
Triathletes, 17

U–V

Unexpected, preparing for the, 65–67
Unfamiliar tasks, 98
Urgency
    avoiding, 51
    defined, 49
Value
    of activities, 13
    of time, changes in, 109, 130
Visitors, 98, 107
Visualizing, 17

W

Waiting, 52, 101, 132
    proverb, 19
Wasted time, 119
Wealth, as goal, 15
Wheel spinning, 78
Working couples, 73–74
Working hours, 2